MARY FORD

Cake Making and Decorating

With step-by-step instructions

The Authors

MARY FORD'S unrivalled skill and infinite patience make her a superb teacher of her craft. Mary has been passing on her expertise for over two decades, through personal contact with students and in her books. During that time she has gained a world-wide reputation for skill and imagination combined with common sense and practical teaching ability. Her unique step-by-step approach, with the emphasis on numerous colour illustrations and brief editorial advice, is ideally suited for introducing beginners and enthusiasts to the skills of cake artistry.

MICHAEL FORD, Mary's husband, collaborates with her in planning and producing the books. All the photographs are taken by him in their studio in Highcliffe. He is also editorial director for the books.

© Copyright Mary Ford Publications Ltd

First published as 'The Concise Book of Cake Making and Decorating' 1988
Reprinted 1990
This edition 1992
Reprinted 1993

Manufactured by Supreme Publishing Services
Printed and bound by star standard, Singapore.

ISBN 0-946429-41-3

Contents

An Introduction to Cake Making and Decorating

In the last twenty years interest in cake making and decorating has increased dramatically. The availability of cake decorating equipment, combined with schools and shops teaching the skills, have helped to bring the craft to a wider audience. Furthermore the beginner and enthusiast have been offered information and advice in a bewildering number of books.

This book 'Cake Making and Decorating' has been written with both the beginner and enthusiast in mind. The Introduction provides information and tips on making the basic cake (in sponge, genoese, fruit etc) and proceeds to explain the alternative coverings. Equipped with this background information the reader can develop their skills on a range of cakes and ideas designed for every occasion all set out with the traditional step-by-step photographs.

Historically, cakes were prepared for Holy Days and Saint's Days and formed a central part of the festivities. We still follow this custom at Easter (with the simnel cake) and at Christmas but the trend has been to celebrate more personal occasions.

The wedding cake in particular has become a major feature of the wedding occasion. It has developed from the 17th century idea of baking small 'bride cakes' which were thrown at the bride for good luck and fertility to the stepped tier cake of the 19th and 20th century. This tiered cake was allegedly the idea of a London pastry cook who modelled the cake on Christopher Wren's new spire for St. Brides Church.

Today we celebrate engagements, birthdays, christenings, retirements, mother and father's days, examination attainments and graduation with a cake, often made and crafted at home by a relative or friend. Sadly, the beautiful work of art is all too briefly admired by the party goers before being cut and consumed.

This book is intended as a guide and reference aid to everyone interested in making, baking and decorating cakes. We hope it will be kept close at hand in the kitchen.

Making a Sponge

fresh egg	3ozs
caster sugar	3ozs
self raising sieved flour	3ozs
hot water	1½ozs

Baking temperature 400°F/204°C or Gas Mark 6

Baking test time 14 minutes

Sponge baking test

When the sponge has been baking for the required time, open oven door slowly and, if sponge is pale in colour, continue baking. When sponge is golden brown, draw fingers across the top of it (lightly pressing and, if this action leaves indentation, continue baking). Repeat test every 2-3 minutes until the top springs back when touched.

Storage instructions

Wrap sponges in waxed paper and store in deep-freeze for up to 6 months. Use within 3 days of cooking (if not frozen) or defrosting.

Chocolate Sponge

Follow the sponge recipe BUT replace ½oz of flour with ½oz of cocoa powder.

Note: ingredients should be 65/70°F when making the sponge

PREPARING A SPONGE TIN
1. Using a pastry brush, grease tin(s) with white fat.

2. Sprinkle sufficient flour into sponge tin to cover base and side.

3. Gently shake and turn tin until all the grease is covered with flour. Then tap out excess flour.

MAKING A SPONGE
1A. Crack open an egg into a small basin before putting into the mixing bowl. Repeat for each egg (to ensure bad doesn't mix with good).

2. Lightly whisk eggs.

3. Pour caster sugar into mixing bowl.

4. Whisk briskly until thick and creamy.

5. Stir-in the 'hot' water.

6. Sprinkle sieved flour on to the mixture.

7. Gently fold in flour with a spatula.

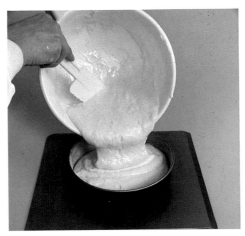

8. Transfer mixture to the prepared tin(s).

9. Place tin(s) near top of pre-heated oven (400°F, 204°C or Gas Mark 6).

10. At end of recommended baking time, test sponge in accordance with the instructions at the top of page 6.

11. After baking, leave to cool for five minutes. Then remove from tin on to greaseproof paper covered in caster sugar.

12. Upturn sponge and place on wire tray until cold. (See instructions for storage – Page 6).

Making a Genoese

Recipe for 10" round or 9" square sponge tin

Additional recipes – page 89

butter	3ozs
margarine	3ozs
caster sugar	6ozs
fresh egg	6ozs
self raising sieved flour	6ozs

Baking temperature 375°F/190°C or Gas Mark 5

Baking test time 20 minutes

Genoese baking test

When the genoese has been baking for the required time, open oven door slowly and, if genoese is pale in colour, continue baking. When genoese is golden brown, draw fingers across the top of it (lightly pressing and, if this action leaves indentation, continue baking). Repeat test every 2-3 minutes until the top springs back when touched.

Storage Instructions

Wrap genoese in waxed paper and store in deep-freeze for up to 6 months. Use within 3 days of cooking (if not frozen) or defrosting.

Chocolate Genoese

Follow the genoese recipe BUT replace 1oz of flour with 1oz of cocoa powder.

Note: ingredients should be 65/70°F when making the genoese

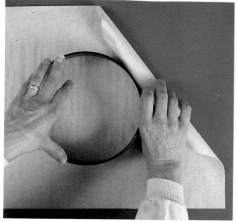

PREPARING A HOOP

1. Place hoop on double sheet of greaseproof paper and roll one corner into side of hoop.

2. Continue rolling paper tightly around the base of the hoop.

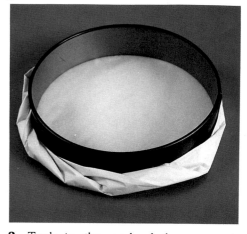

3. Tuck in the end of the paper to complete hoop base, then place on baking sheet. Grease inside of hoop and base lightly with white fat.

PREPARING A TIN

1. Using sponge tin, mark and then cut out a disc of greaseproof paper.

2. Using a pastry brush, grease tin(s) with white fat.

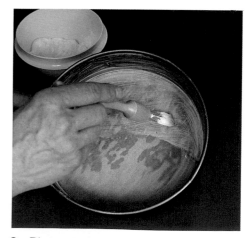

3. Place greaseproof paper disc into bottom of the tin and brush over with white fat.

MAKING A GENOESE

1. Mix, then beat the margarine and butter until soft and light.

2. Beat in caster sugar to form a fluffy consistency. (Now test eggs – Page 6, No.1A).

3. Thoroughly beat in a small portion of egg at a time until all egg is used.

4. Pour sieved flour on to mixture.

5. Gently fold flour into mixture. (Don't overmix).

6. Spoon mixture into prepared hoop(s) or tin(s).

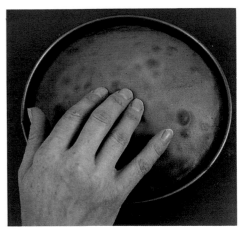

7. Evenly spread mixture with a spatula.

8. Place tin(s) at centre of pre-heated oven (375°F/190°C or Gas Mark 5).

9. At end of recommended baking time, test genoese in accordance with the instructions at the top of page 8. After baking, see Nos. 11-12 on page 7.

Making a Fruit Cake
Basic Recipe

	Imperial / Metric	American
plain flour	2ozs / 57g	½ cup
brown sugar	2ozs / 57g	⅓ cup
butter	2ozs / 57g	¼ cup
currants	2½ozs / 71g	½ cup
sultanas	2½ozs / 71g	½ cup
seedless raisins	1oz / 28g	3 tblspn
glacé cherries	1oz / 28g	3 tblspn
mixed peel	1½ozs / 42g	4½ tblspn
ground almonds	¾oz / 21g	2½ tblspn
brandy or rum	½fl oz / 2 tspn	2 tspn
large fresh eggs	1 egg / 1 egg	1 egg
nutmeg	1 pinch / 1 pinch	1 pinch
mixed spice	1 pinch / 1 pinch	1 pinch
salt	1 pinch / 1 pinch	1 pinch
lemon zest & juice	¼ lemon / ¼ lemon	¼ lemon

Soaking mixture
Equal quantities of rum, sherry and glycerine or spirits of choice. 1 tablespoon per 1lb of cake when required.

Cake portions
To calculate size of fruit cake required 8 portions are generally cut from each 1lb of finished iced cake.

Dark Fruit Cake
A darker fruit cake can be achieved by substituting 10% of the sugar with black treacle.

Cake Baking Instructions
At the end of the recommended baking time, test the cake to ensure it is properly cooked by –
 (a) bringing the cake forward from the oven;
 (b) inserting a steel skewer into the cake's centre;
 (c) slowly raise skewer and, if clean, the cake is baked and should be removed from the oven; if mixture clings to the skewer, remove skewer and continue baking at the same temperature. Test thereafter at 10 minute intervals until the cake is baked.

Fruit Cake – Storage
Place wrapped cake in a cool dry atmosphere which allows odourless air circulation out of direct sunlight.
If not stored correctly the cake could become mouldy because of –
 (a) being wrapped whilst still warm;
 (b) a quality waxed paper was not used in wrapping the cake;
 (c) it is stored in the wrong temperature or in a variable temperature;
 (d) the presence of moisture in the air;
 (e) under-baking;
 (f) too much soaking with alcohol after baking;
 (g) leaving the cake too long before wrapping it in waxed paper.

DO NOT STORE cakes in – sealed plastic containers, cling-film or tin-foil.

To prevent the cake cracking whilst being handled, wrap and then immediately place on a cake-board.

Deep Freeze Storage – Fruit Cake
Although it is not really necessary to freeze a quality baked fruit cake, such a cake can be frozen. A decorated fruit cake should not be frozen unless the marzipan/almond paste and royal icing/sugar paste has been first removed.

CAKE SIZES AND QUANTITIES WITH APPROXIMATE BAKING TIMES
The quantities stated in the basic recipe shown above should be multiplied by the figures shown below for the various cake tin shapes.

Basic Fruit Cake Recipe
(Bake at 275°F, 140°C, Gas Mark 1)

Cake Tin Size (ins)	Cake Tin Shape (Basic recipe multiplied by...)				Approx Timing (hrs)
	Round	Square	Heart	Hexagonal	
5	1	1½	1½	1	1½ – 1¾
6	1½	2	2	1½	1¾ – 2
7	2	3	3	2	2½ – 3
8	3	4	4	3	3½ – 4
9	4	5	5	4	4 – 4½
10	5	6	6	5	4¼ – 4¾
11	6	7	7	6	4½ – 5
12	7	8	8	7	5 – 5½

Note: See page 88 for AT-A-GLANCE INGREDIENT QUANTITIES CONVERSION

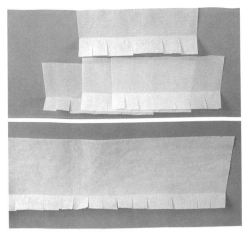

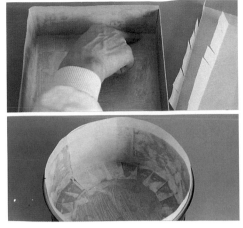

PREPARING A CAKE TIN

1. Cut greaseproof paper 2″ deeper than cake-tin to cover side(s). (4 pieces for square tin and 1 piece for round tin).

2. Grease tin then cover side(s) and 1″ around base with the prepared greaseproof paper. Also ensure paper is 1″ above tin height.

3. Cut greaseproof paper and fit into base of tin, then grease.

PREPARING CAKE INGREDIENTS

1. Weigh ingredients on separate sheets of greaseproof paper, using recipe on page 10.

2. Inspect and clean fruit and then chop cherries in half.

3. Grate the lemon and put the zest with the fruit and liquor into a bowl and thoroughly mix.

4. Thoroughly mix and sieve flour, salt and spices on to greaseproof paper several times.

5. Crack open an egg into a small basin before putting into the mixing bowl. Repeat for each egg (to ensure bad doesn't mix with good).

6. Leave all ingredients in a warm room for 12 hours (65°F or 18°C).

MAKING A CAKE
1. Beat butter until light.

2. Add and beat-in sugar until light.

3. Thoroughly beat-in a small portion of egg at a time until all egg is used.

4. Stir-in the ground almonds.

5. Add flour and spices to mixture.

6. Fold flour and spices lightly into mixture and mix until clear.

7. Add fruit and liquor.

8. Add lemon juice to mixture.

9. Stir mixture thoroughly, but **DO NOT BEAT.**

10. Spoon required quantity of mixture into prepared cake tin(s).

11. Dip hand in luke warm water and then flatten mixture with the back of wet hand.

12. Place cake-tin in centre of pre-heated oven (275°F, 140°C or Gas Mark 1) – with oven-proof bowl containing water beneath.

13. At half the baking time, remove water from oven.

14. At end of recommended baking time test cake in accordance with instructions at the top of page 10.

15. When cake is baked, remove from oven and leave in cool place for 24 hours in the tin.

16. Prepare soaking mixture (See page 10).

17. Carefully remove greaseproof paper from cake. Upturn cake and brush on soaking mixture (one tablespoon per pound of cake).

18. Wrap cake in waxed paper, date it and store cake to mature. (See page 10 for storage instructions).

Making Buttercream

Recipes

	Imperial/Metric	American
butter	6ozs/170g	¾ cup
sieved icing sugar	12ozs/341g	2⅔ cups
warm water	3 tblspns/3 tblspns	3 tblspns

Note: All ingredients should be 65/70°F when making the buttercream.

1. Soften butter and beat until light.

2. Gradually add the sieved icing sugar (beating well after each addition).

3. Add and beat in water (and colour and flavour if required).

Making Almond Paste

Recipes

	Imperial/Metric	American
sieved icing sugar	16ozs/454g	3½ cups
ground sweet almonds	8ozs/227g	1¾ cups
egg yolks (approx. number)	4/4	4

For a gritty texture use half caster sugar and half icing sugar.

Note: Yellow food colouring may be added if desired. The consistency of the paste can be adjusted by increasing or decreasing the amount of egg yolk used.

Note: All ingredients should be 65/70°F when making the almond paste.

1. Mix dry ingredients together.

2. Mix egg yolks and add to the dry ingredients.

3. Knead mixture until pliable.

Making Albumen Solution

Recipes

	Imperial/Metric	American
pure albumen powder	1oz/26g	⅛ cup
water	6ozs/170g	¾ cup

1. Pour water into bowl and stir whilst sprinkling in the dried albumen.

2. Thoroughly mix. Stir occasionally during next hour.

3. Strain mixture, which is now ready for use, through sieve or muslin.

Making Royal Icing

Recipes

	Imperial/Metric	American
fresh egg whites or albumen solution	3ozs/85g	⅜ cup
sieved icing sugar or confectioners sugar	16ozs/454g	3 cups

Note: Separate fresh egg whites 24 hours before required.

Glycerine – Table for use

For soft-cutting icing (per 1lb or 454g or 3½ cups of ready-made royal icing) use 1 teaspoon of glycerine for the bottom tier of a 3-tier wedding cake. 2 teaspoons of glycerine for the middle tier. 3 teaspoons of glycerine for the top tier, or for single tier cakes.

1. Place albumen solution or fresh egg-white into bowl.

2. Stir and beat-in ⅓rd of the icing sugar with the egg white or albumen solution. Repeat until all icing sugar is used.

3. Beat mixture until light and fluffy and peaks can be formed. Scrape inside of bowl and cover with a damp cloth. Use when required.

(N.B. Glycerine only to be added after royal icing has been made.)
NO GLYCERINE IN ROYAL ICING FOR RUNOUTS OR No.1 WORK.

Making Sugar Paste

Recipes

	Imperial/Metric	American
sieved icing sugar	16ozs/454g	3½ cups
egg white	1/1	1
warm glucose	2ozs/57g	4 tblspns

Sugar paste is firm, unheated and sweet and is generally rolled out into sheet form (in a similar manner to marzipan/almond paste) to cover cakes. It is also used – as illustrated on page 51 – for making flowers, animals, frills, etc. Sugar paste can be coloured and flavoured to suit personal choice.

Note: Separate fresh egg whites 24 hours before required.

1. Warm bowl containing glucose in a saucepan of hot water.

2. Sieve icing sugar.

3. Place icing sugar and egg-white into mixing bowl.

4. Add warmed glucose.

5. Mix thoroughly.

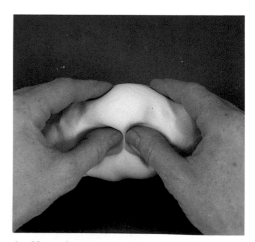

6. Knead mixture to a pliable paste, then wrap in a polythene bag and store in a cool place.

Recipes

	Imperial/Metric	American
cube sugar	32ozs/908g	10 cups
water	10ozs/284g	2 cups
glucose	6ozs/170g	1½ cups

Stock Syrup *Recipe*

	Imperial/Metric	American
caster sugar	8ozs/227g	2 cups
water	10ozs/284g	2½ cups

To make fondant, follow instructions below Nos.1-12. After storage and when required, reheat to 100°F (38°C) to achieve a pouring consistency. Fondant is then ideal for covering small tea fancies and sponge cakes. When melted, it can be coloured and flavoured as required.

Bring to the boil. Remove from heat, leave to cool then use as required.

Temperature Comparison
100°F (38°C)
225°F (107°C)
240°F (116°C)

1. Lightly oil bars and marble slab over an area of 18″ × 18″ (for each 2lbs of sugar).

2. Place cube sugar and water into saucepan and heat until sugar dissolves – DO NOT BOIL.

3. At 225°F, remove spoon, pour in the warmed glucose and bring to boil – DO NOT STIR.

4. During boiling brush water on inside of saucepan to prevent crystallisation.

5. Continue fast boiling to 240°F.

6. At 240°F, remove saucepan and place it in a bowl of cold water for 2 minutes.

7. Pour the mixture on to the prepared part of the marble slab. DO NOT SCRAPE OUT SAUCEPAN on to the slab.

8. Allow to cool to 100°F.

9. AT 100°F remove bars and with a palette knife start to turn the mixture.

10. As the mixture thickens to a white mass, use a palette knife in each hand. Continue turning until mixture is cold.

11. Cover the mixture (fondant) with a damp cloth for 30 minutes.

12. Now mix the fondant for another 5 minutes, transfer it to a sealed container and store in a cool place.

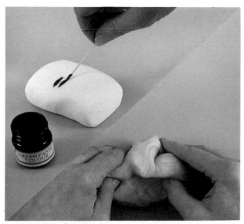

COLOURING ROYAL ICING

To avoid overcolouring, add colour to a small portion of royal icing and then add to the full amount. Repeat process until correct colour is obtained.

If blue does *not* form any part of the colouring to be used, DO NOT USE BLUE when making the royal icing.

COLOURING SUGAR PASTE OR MARZIPAN/ALMOND PASTE

Dip a cocktail stick into the food-colour of choice and wipe on to the paste. Then repeatedly fold the paste by hand until the colour is thoroughly mixed in.

COLOURING/FLAVOURING BUTTERCREAM

Add artificial flavouring, or strained fruit, or zest of fruit, or melted chocolate to the buttercream and then add and thoroughly mix in a complimentary food colour. *CAUTION – do not overcolour.*

If mixture starts to curdle immediately add more buttercream (or more icing sugar).

Using Colour in Cake Decoration

The reason for adding colour in cake decoration is to give the end result *eye* appeal. However, it is important to remember that whatever colours you choose, the general overall appearance of the cake must remain enticing.

Most colours used in cake decoration (with the exception of chocolate and coffee) tend to be pale pastel shades. Stronger colours usually indicate a bitter taste so these should be used sparingly for contrast and to ensure harmony.

When colouring your mixture always work in daylight. Mix up a small quantity on a tabletop and transfer it to the bulk of the mixture.

When adding colouring to royal icing or sugar paste, remember that you can always add more colouring if necessary — you can never take it away! Add the colouring cautiously, a little at a time, checking the tone as you progress with the mixing. Too much too soon can often result in a much darker tone than is required.

Flavour to Colour

White	—	vanilla, maraschino
Pink	—	raspberry, strawberry, cherry, rose water
Lemon	—	lemon, pineapple
Orange	—	orange, curacao
Green	—	peppermint, lime, almond

Note: When using a flavouring to colour icing it is essential to taste the mixture as you progress.

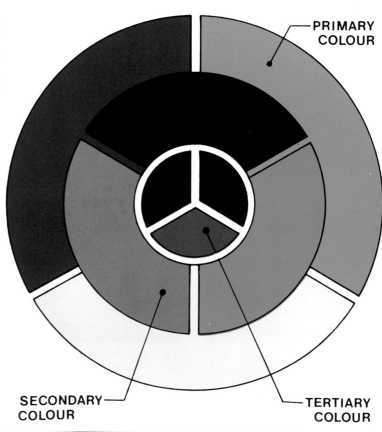

PRIMARY COLOUR

SECONDARY COLOUR

TERTIARY COLOUR

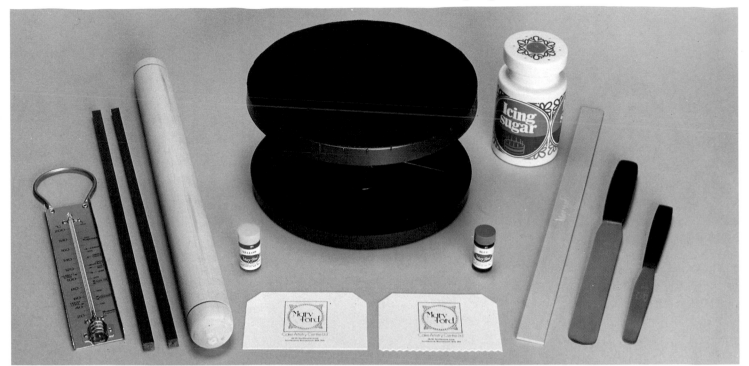

EDIBLE FOOD COLOURS 1

The law requires certain attributes in food colouring and this should be complied with. Such requirements preclude the use of certain fixing agents and, therefore, fading is now more likely to occur.

As colouring is so important to the end product, it is advisable to test the colour(s) being used in a small quantity of royal icing, buttercream, sugar paste, fondant etc.

ICING SUGAR 2

Sugarcraft decoration relies on good quality icing sugar, such as that supplied by Tate and Lyle.

LARGE PALETTE KNIFE 3

The most suitable palette knife for coating cakes should have a 7 inch stainless steel firm blade and a welded comfortable handle.

ROLLING PIN 4

A suitable rolling pin for rolling out pastes should be about 18 inches long, 1½ inches in diameter, of smooth surface and of a good weight.

SCRAPERS 5

Scrapers can be obtained in a variety of patterns. Their main use is to smooth royal icing or buttercream around the sides of cakes. Each scraper should be comfortable to hold, slightly flexible and have good clean-cut facing edges.

SMALL PALETTE KNIFE 6

The ideal palette knife for mixing colour into small quantities of royal icing (and other similar uses) should have a 4 inch stainless steel firm blade and a welded comfortable handle.

SPACERS 7

A spacer placed each side of paste will ensure consistent thickness of the paste when rolled with a rolling pin. The ideal spacer is made of nylon, 15 inches long and ⅜ inch square.

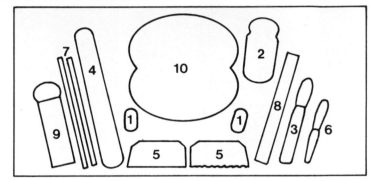

STRAIGHT EDGE 8

This instrument is used for smoothing royal icing or buttercream on cake-tops. It must be rigid, have smooth edges and be some 15 inches long. A non-ferrous metal is the best medium.

SUGAR BOILING THERMOMETER 9

When making fondant, it is necessary to obtain a reading of the sugar's temperature with a thermometer. A good thermometer for the purpose has – a strong back support for the glass rod; a well protected bulb; easily readable markings; highly visible liquid gauge; and a firm large handle.

TURNTABLE 10

A good turntable –
(a) is constructed so as to be capable of supporting a large cake without affecting the turntable's mobility;
(b) has a minimum diameter of 9 inches, to enable safe carriage of a loaded 20 inch diameter cake-board;
(c) will always have sufficient space between its base and top – of at least 3 inches – to enable the decorator to easily rotate the turntable;
(d) must have a non-slip top and base; and
(e) will give continual smooth rotation if the spindle is regularly greased with edible oil.

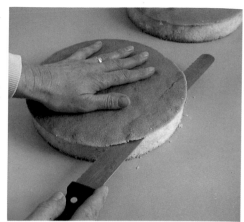

PREPARING AND FILLING A GENOESE

1. Add to buttercream and mix, artificial flavour or strained fruit juice of choice.

2. Now add and thoroughly mix-in complimentary food colour.

3. Remove top crust from two genoese bases.

4. Upturn and remove bottom crust from genoese.

5. Slice each base in half whilst holding top firmly.

6. Place one slice on cake-board and cover top with a preserve (jam).

7. Add second slice and cover top with buttercream.

8. Add third slice and cover top with a preserve.

9. Add last slice with gentle pressure.

GENOESE/SPONGE – FIRST COAT OF BUTTERCREAM

1. Spread buttercream over the filled genoese (or sponge) top.

2. Using a level palette knife, smooth buttercream by rotating genoese on a turntable.

3. Spread buttercream around side of genoese with a palette knife.

4. Smooth side with a plain scraper whilst turning genoese on the turntable.

5. Remove surplus buttercream from top edge with a palette knife.

6. Place coated genoese in refrigerator for one hour before giving final coat. (See page 22).

ALTERNATIVE METHOD OF FIRST COATING

1. Place filled genoese (or sponge) on cake-card of same size and hold as shown. Spread buttercream on side.

2. Smooth side and then spread surplus buttercream on to sponge top with a palette knife.

3. Add more buttercream to cake-top and smooth with palette knife. Place in refrigerator for one hour before giving final coat. (See page 22).

GENOESE/SPONGE – FINAL COATING

1. Apply second coat of buttercream to genoese (or sponge) top.

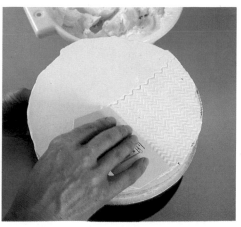

2. Draw a serrated scraper in a zig-zag motion across one-half of genoese top, if required.

3. Smooth side with a plain scraper whilst turning genoese on a turntable.

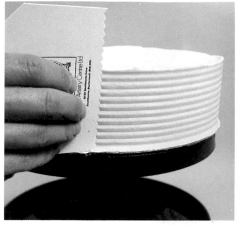

4. Picture showing use of serrated scraper (steadily held against side).

5. Picture showing use of serrated scraper (being used in a wavy motion whilst genoese is being turned).

SAMPLE COVERINGS

1. Hold coated genoese in palm of hand.

2. Fill other hand with vermicelli and palm it on to lower half of genoese side.

2a. OR cover side with roasted nibbed almonds.

2b. OR cover whole genoese with roasted flaked almonds.

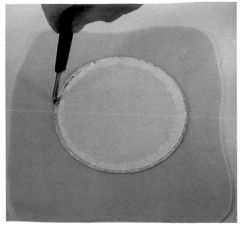

GENOESE/SPONGE – DECORATED DESIGN

1. Fill and apply first coat to genoese (or sponge). (See pages 20-21).

2. Roll out and cut a disc of sugar paste to match the size of the coated sponge (using a cake-card as a guide).

3. Remove surplus sugar paste and slide the cake-card under the disc.

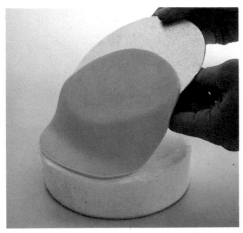

4. Now remove the disc from the cake-card by sliding it directly in position on the sponge-top.

5. Cover sponge-side with chopped nuts or other covering of choice.

6. Decorate sponge with sugar paste hearts and a personal message in piped royal icing.

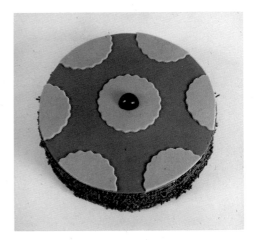

ALTERNATIVE DESIGNS

1A. A sugar paste flower with piped buttercream stems and leaves, leaving space for message of choice.

1B. Pipe royal icing lines to form a pair of storks and cut out sugar paste flowers.

1C. Cut out sugar paste discs and place on sponge-top, as shown.

NOTE: Almond paste can be used instead of marzipan.

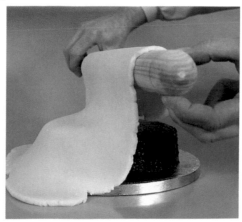

COVERING A FRUIT CAKE WITH SUGAR PASTE

1. Fill in cake imperfections with marzipan and then brush boiling apricot purée over whole top and side.

2. Roll out sufficient marzipan to cover the top and side. Lift marzipan with rolling pin and place it over the cake.

3. Roughly trim marzipan, if necessary, to cake-board edge. Now, using the palm of the hand, push marzipan to the cake-side.

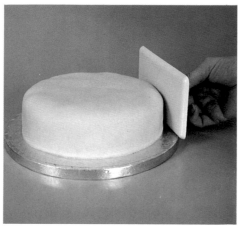

4. Trim surplus marzipan from cake-base by keeping the knife tight against the cake-side.

5. Flatten and smooth entire marzipan surface with a cake-smoother.

6. Brush whole surface with a clear alcohol (e.g. gin or vodka).

7. Immediately repeat Nos. 2-5 using sugar paste. Leave to crust, then the cake is ready to decorate.

COVERING A GENOESE, OR SPONGE WITH SUGAR PASTE

1. Fill and coat a genoese (or sponge). (See pages 20-21).

2. Cover coated genoese in accordance with instructions Nos. 2-5 above, **BUT USING SUGAR PASTE** and not marzipan.

COATING A SPONGE-TOP WITH FONDANT

1. Warm fondant to 100°F in a bain-marie. Add stock syrup, colour and flavour to achieve consistency shown.

2. Fill a sponge with jam, thinly cover top with boiling apricot purée and then spoon-on warmed fondant.

3. Immediately spread fondant evenly over sponge-top. Leave to cool for 20 minutes. Decorate as required.

COMPLETELY COATING A SPONGE WITH FONDANT

1. Fill and cover a sponge with sugar paste or marzipan.

2. Brush covering all over with boiling apricot purée and then place sponge on to a wire tray.

3. Warm, colour and flavour sufficient fondant to cover whole sponge. (See No.1. above). Pour fondant on to cake-top.

4. Immediately spread fondant over the sponge-top with a palette knife.

5. Continue spreading the fondant around the sponge-side. Leave to cool for 20 minutes.

6. Dip palette knife into warm water and then immediately trim and remove sponge from wire tray and place on a cake-board. Decorate as required.

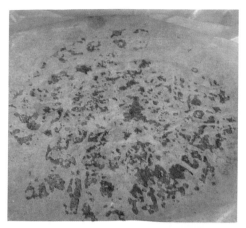

MARZIPANNING A CAKE-TOP
1. Picture showing colour of waxed paper containing matured fruit cake.

2. Remove waxed paper, place cake on board and, if required, brush on more soaking mixture. (1 teaspoon per 1lb of cake).

3. Dust worktable and marzipan with icing sugar (between two spacers).

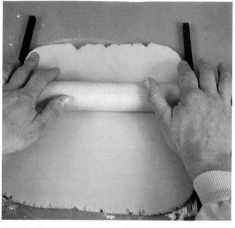

4. Roll marzipan with heavy rolling pin on spacers (which will give an even thickness).

5. Cut marzipan (for cake-top) to size using the cake tin in which the cake was baked as a guide.

6. Thinly spread boiled apricot purée over cake-top.

7. Upturn cake on to marzipan and trim as necessary.

8. Return cake to board and brush off surplus icing sugar from cake-top.

9. Cover cake-side in waxed paper and leave for 3 days. Then coat and decorate as required.

NOTE: Boiled apricot purée should always be used whilst still hot.

LAYERING A CAKE WITH MARZIPAN

1. Picture showing matured cake on cake-board.

2. Slice cake in half (using a sharp scalloped knife).

3. Place top half of cake on a thin cake-board and brush soaking mixture on to the top of each half (1 teaspoon per 1lb of cake). Leave for 24 hours.

4. Thinly spread boiled apricot purée over top of cake on the thick cake-board.

5. Roll-out, cut and place marzipan, as shown, on cake-top.

6. Thinly spread boiled apricot purée over marzipan, after brushing off surplus icing sugar.

7. Place other half of cake on top of marzipan and then spread boiled apricot purée on top.

8. Roll-out, cut and place marzipan on cake-top, as shown.

9. Brush off surplus icing sugar from cake-top. (See page 28 for marzipanning the cake-side *or* page 26, No.9).

NOTE: Boiled apricot purée should always be used whilst still hot.

MARZIPANNING THE SIDE OF A ROUND CAKE

1. Dust worktable and marzipan with icing sugar. Roll marzipan into sausage shape (three times the width of the cake).

2. Using a rolling pin, roll out the marzipan into a thin strip (wide enough to cover the cake-side).

3. Cut marzipan to exact depth of cake and then thinly spread boiled apricot purée over the marzipan.

4. Roll cake on to the marzipan, as shown, lining up edge with base of cake.

5. Trim surplus marzipan off top edge. Leave to dry for 3 days, then coat *or* immediately cut a wedge.

CUTTING A WEDGE

1. Using a sharp knife, mark an appropriate sized wedge shape into cake-top marzipan.

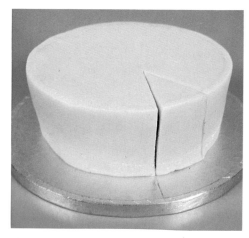

2. Continue marking wedge shape down side of cake and on cake-board, as shown.

3. Following marks, cut out wedge using a sharp scalloped knife (without cutting into board surface).

4. Replace wedge and leave cake to dry for three days before coating.

Note: Boiled apricot purée should always be used whilst still hot.

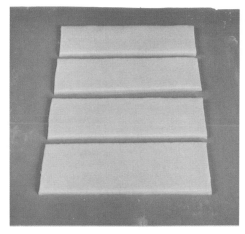

MARZIPANNING A SQUARE CAKE
1. Follow instructions on page 26 (1-8) to marzipan cake-top.

2. Roll out enough marzipan to cover cake sides (using icing sugar for dusting).

3. Cut marzipan into four strips (each being equal to the width and depth of the cake-side).

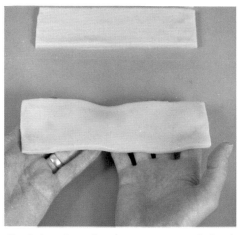

4. Thinly spread boiled apricot purée over each length of marzipan.

5. Lift a length of marzipan with both hands.

6. Press marzipan to cake-side and firm in. Repeat for each side.

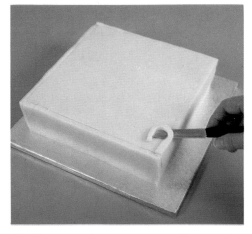

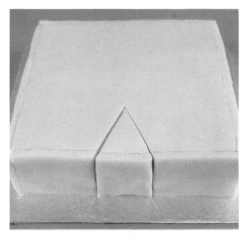

7. Trim surplus marzipan off top edge and from each corner. Leave to dry for 3 days, then coat *or* immediately cut a wedge.

CUTTING A WEDGE
1. Cut wedge (in manner shown on page 28), if required.

2. Replace wedge and leave cake to dry for three days before coating.

Note: Boiled apricot purée should always be used whilst still hot.

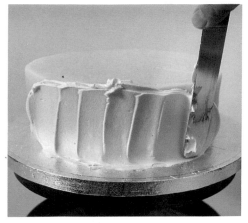

COATING A ROUND CAKE
1. Place a quantity of royal icing on cake-side with a palette knife.

2. Spread icing around cake-side, adding more icing as necessary. Ensure cake-side is fully covered.

3. Place hands in position shown (holding a scraper against cake-side).

4. Holding scraper steady with one hand, revolve the turntable one complete turn with other hand. Repeat until side is smooth.

5. Using a palette knife, remove surplus icing from the top edge of the cake and from the cake-board.

6. Immediately remove the wedge, if there is one.

7. Remove surplus icing from wedge and wedge cavity. Replace wedge and leave to dry for 12 hours.

8. With a palette knife place some royal icing on top of the cake.

9. Spread the icing over the cake-top, adding more icing as necessary. Ensure cake-top is fully covered.

Note: Royal icing should be made 24 hours before use. See 'glycerine-table for use' for soft cutting icing on page 15.

10. Use a metal rule in a full forwards and backwards motion until the icing on the cake-top is completely smooth.

11. Using a palette knife, remove surplus icing from the cake-top edge.

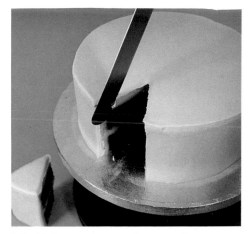

12. Take out wedge and remove surplus icing. Replace wedge. Leave to dry for 12 hours. Repeat 1-12 twice more, thus giving three coats.

FIXING WEDGE RIBBON

13. Place 1½ yards of satin ribbon centrally across greaseproof paper measuring 8 × 6 inches.

14. Fold the greaseproof paper over the ribbon, as shown.

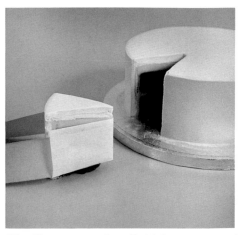

15. Remove wedge. Fold the paper and ribbon in half and place around wedge. Replace wedge.

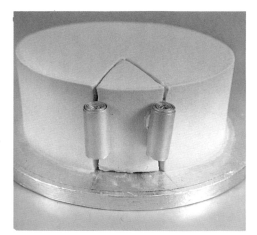

16. Roll up equal lengths of ribbon-ends and fix to cake-side with royal icing, then coat board *or* decorate.

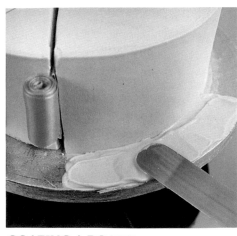

COATING A BOARD

1. Spread royal icing on cake-board using a palette knife.

2. Holding scraper steady in position shown, turn turntable with other hand until icing is smooth. Leave to dry for 12 hours. Decorate as required.

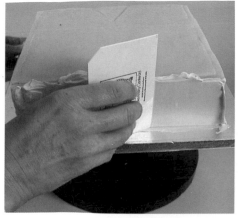

COATING A SQUARE CAKE

1. Fully cover one cake-side, with royal icing. Now repeatedly draw scraper along that side until icing is smooth.

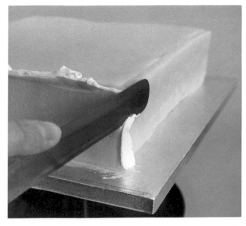

2. Remove surplus icing from each corner, by using a palette knife in the manner shown.

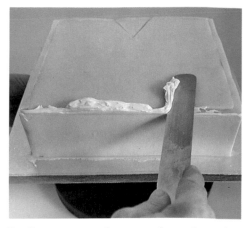

3. Remove surplus icing from the cake-top edge, by using a palette knife in the manner shown.

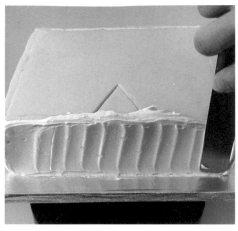

4. Repeat 1-3 on the opposite side of the cake. Leave to dry for 12 hours.

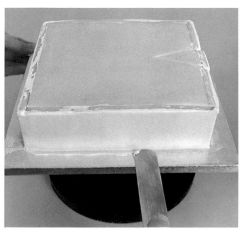

5. Repeat 1-3 on the third side and then again on the fourth side. Leave to dry for 12 hours.

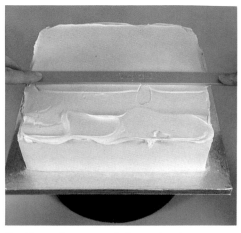

6. Coat the top of the cake (see pages 30-31, Nos. 8-10).

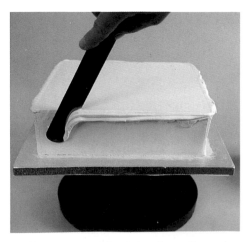

7. Remove surplus icing from the cake-top edge with a palette knife. Leave to dry for 12 hours.

8. Repeat 1-7 twice more, thus giving three coats. *If cake has a wedge, remove wedge immediately after each coat. (See wedge instructions on pages 30-31).*

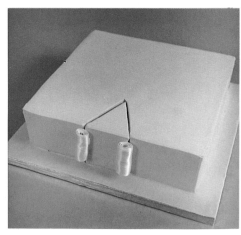

9. If relevant, fix wedge ribbon (Page 31, Nos. 13-16). Coat board (page 31, Nos. 1-2).

Note: Royal icing should be made 24 hours before use. See 'glycerine-table for use' for soft cutting icing on page 15.

If cake has wedge, follow wedge instructions on pages 30-31 Nos. 6, 7, 12-16.

ALTERNATIVE (QUICK) METHOD OF COATING A CAKE

1. Spread royal icing over cake-top and, with a metal rule, smooth with a full forward and backward motion.

2. Bring surplus icing down to cover the side, adding more as necessary. Using a scraper, smooth the side by rotating the turntable.

3. Remove surplus icing from cake-top edge and base. Leave to dry for 12 hours. Repeat Nos. 1-3 twice more. Then coat cake-board. (See page 31, Nos. 1-2).

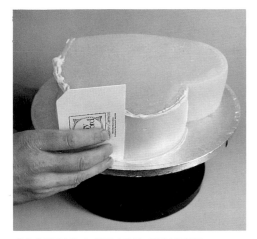 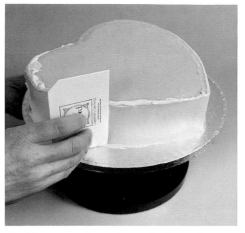 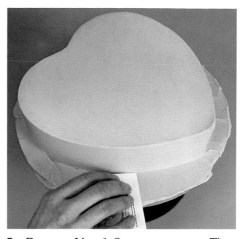

COATING A HEART-SHAPED CAKE

1. Starting from the back, coat one side to the front of the cake with royal icing.

2. Now coat the other side from front to back. Leave to dry for 12 hours. Coat the top of the cake (see pages 30-31, Nos. 8-10). Leave to dry for 12 hours.

3. Repeat Nos.1-2 twice more. Then coat cake-board. (See page 31, Nos. 17-18).

 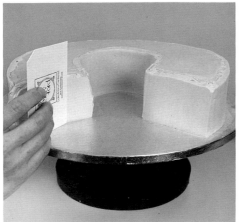 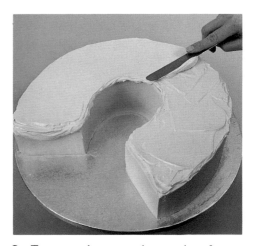

COATING A HORSESHOE-SHAPED CAKE

1. Coat and smooth outside of the cake with royal icing, using a scraper. Then coat and smooth the inside of the horseshoe with an upright palette knife.

2. Leave to dry for 12 hours. Coat and smooth cake-top using a palette knife.

3. Trim surplus icing from edge. Leave to dry for 12 hours.
Repeat Nos. 1-3 twice more. Decorate as required.

Note: Royal icing should be made 24 hours before use. See 'glycerine-table for use' for soft cutting icing on page 15.

33

Cake Shapes

Contrary to popular belief, it is not necessary to own numerous cake tins to obtain different shapes. For example, the following patterns can easily be produced from either a round, or, as the case may be, square cake. Although each of the examples are genoese cakes, they can equally be sponge or fruit cake.

Obviously, clean cutting is essential for the overall appearance of the cake and, therefore, it is strongly recommended that a long, strong, sharp and scalloped knife be used for the purpose. It is also important to always cut on a firm surface.

An alternative method of making an open book shape, is to bake the cake in a small clean meat tin (with sloping sides). Only the centre 'V' then needs to be removed.

Additional cake shapes, especially for children's birthdays, can be extracted from their books.

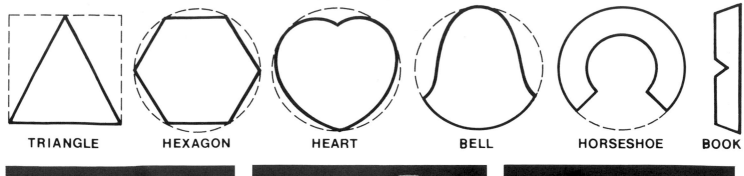

TRIANGLE   HEXAGON   HEART   BELL   HORSESHOE   BOOK

1. Place a paper triangle on a square cake and cut off each side. Join the cut pieces together to form a diamond-shaped cake.

2. Place a paper hexagon on a round cake and cut off each side to form a hexagon-shaped cake.

3. Place a paper heart on a round cake and cut off surplus cake to form a heart-shaped cake.

4. Place a paper bell on a round cake and cut off each side to form a bell-shaped cake.

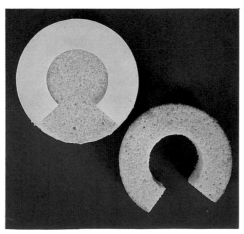

5. Place a paper horseshoe on a round cake and cut out centre of cake to form a horseshoe-shaped cake.

6. Place a paper book-shape edge at the end of a square sponge. Cut and remove a 'V' shaped wedge from the centre and then angle each side to form a book-shaped cake.

Roll out and cut sugar paste (to fit a round coated sponge/cake) in the shape of one of the following numbers and place on cake-top. There is no need to cut the sponge/cake and, therefore, no cake wastage. It is recommended that royal icing be used for all piped work on this page.

1. These contrasting colours emphasise the importance of the occasion. Piped bulbs and lines create simple elegance.

2. These colours suit a boy or girl's second birthday. Large scrolls and shells around the cake's edge complete a strong design.

3. Kenny's candle cars 'race' around the No.3 track and should bring excitement to any three-year old.

4. Airport runways and radar lines are the basis of this 4th birthday cake. Piped dots indicate landing lights.

5. Strident colours add to the tone of this five-year old's 'musical' cake.

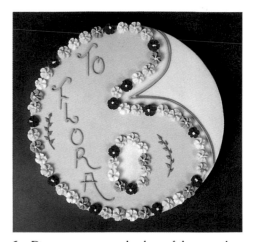

6. Pipe stars around edge of the number '6' to form a pretty floral border and then pipe a dot in the centre of each star.

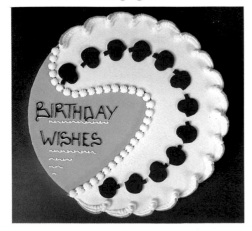

7. Love for a seven-year old is expressed through the sugar paste chain of hearts. Delicate piping adds to the daintiness of the occasion.

8. The sophisticated simplicity of this cake is enhanced by carefully balanced royal icing piping.

9. Strong bright colours dominate the number '9' age group and are supported by curved lines and bulbs.

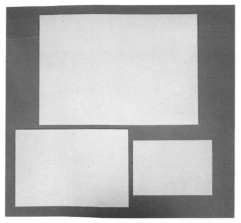

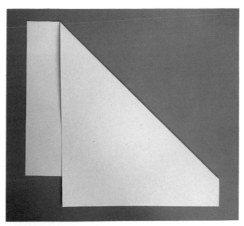

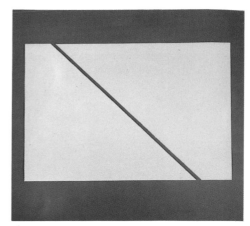

MAKING A GREASEPROOF PAPER PIPING BAG

1. Cut greaseproof for:- Large bags – 18″ × 14″; Medium bags – 14″ × 10″; Small bags – 10″ × 8″.

2. Whichever size of bag to be used, fold paper as shown.

3. Cut along crease (to form two identical shapes), as shown.

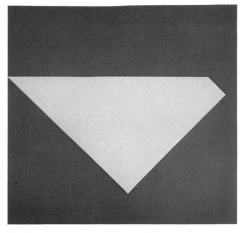

4. Turn one piece of paper to the position shown.

5. Pick up the top right corner and start to curl it towards the centre.

6. Continue curling to the position shown and hold firmly to form a cone.

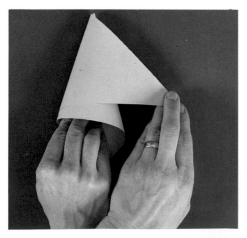

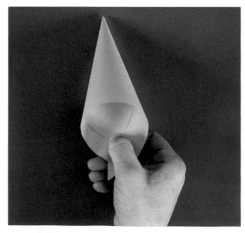

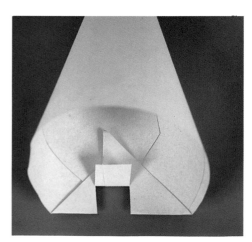

7. Now, with the other hand, lift the opposite corner completely over cone.

8. Continue curling paper under the cone and pull taut until a sharp point is formed at tip.

9. Fold in loose ends and cut and fold the small section shown (to secure the bag).

(Note: To aid definition, blue coloured paper has been used).

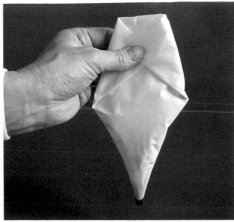

FILLING AND HOLDING A PIPING BAG

1. Cut tip off bag to hold icing tube. Drop tube in and, using a palette knife, half fill bag with royal icing.

2. Flatten the wide part of the bag and gently squeeze icing down to the tube. Fold each side of the bag to the centre.

3. Roll the wide end of the bag towards the tube to seal the bag.

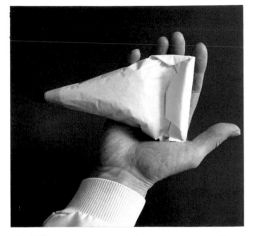

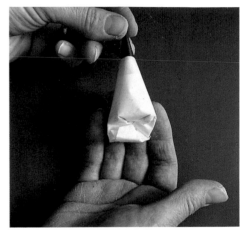

4. When using a large or medium greaseproof paper bag, place bag into the centre of hand, as shown.

5. Grip bag and place thumb over wide end, ready for piping.

6. When using a small bag, rest bag on finger tips, as shown.

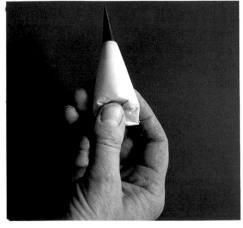

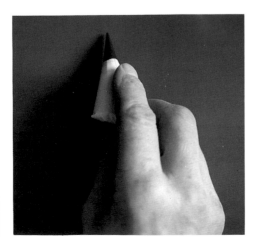

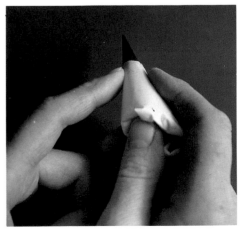

7. Secure bag by gripping it with fingers and thumb.

8. Now turn the bag over and then place the first finger in line with the icing tube.

9. Prior to piping, steady the bag with both hands.

Piped Shapes

Using a Course Star Tube with either royal icing or buttercream.

(Note: Any Star piping tube may be used to achieve similar piped shapes).

1. STAR. Hold piping bag still in a vertical position and press.

2. At required size, stop pressing and lift bag upright.

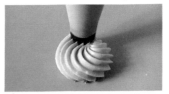

3. ROSETTE. Press upright bag whilst turning in a clockwise motion.

4. On completion of one turn stop pressing and draw bag away.

5. 'C' LINE. Pipe in anti-clockwise and upward direction.

6. Form tail, stop piping and slide tube on surface.

7. LATERAL 'C' LINE. Pipe in anti-clockwise direction at an even height to form first curve.

8. Continue piping to form the matching curve. Stop piping and lift bag upright.

9. SKEIN. Pipe in anti-clockwise direction at an even height to form the first curve.

10. Continue piping in clockwise direction to form matching curve. Stop piping and lift bag upright.

11. REVERSE SKEIN. Pipe in a clockwise direction at an even height to form the first curve.

12. Continue piping in anti-clockwise direction and stop when the matching opposite curve is complete, then lift bag upright.

13. SHELL. Hold piping bag at the angle shown and start to press.

14. Continue pressing, whilst lifting bag.

15. Continue pressing until required size.

16. Stop pressing, then slide tube down along surface to form tail.

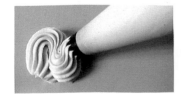

17. ZIGZAG LINE. Pipe in tight waves whilst keeping tube on surface.

18. Continue piping an even zigzag. Stop piping and slide tube away.

19. ROPE. Pipe spring-shape in clockwise direction, using even pressure and keeping bag horizontal.

20. Continue piping in a straight even pattern. Stop piping and pull bag away in a half-turn.

Before attempting to pipe any one shape, please study the whole sequence of photographs and notes for that shape.

21. CONVEX ROPE. Pipe spring-shape in clockwise direction, using even pressure and keeping bag horizontal.

22. Continue piping to form the curve shown. Stop piping and pull bag away in a half-turn.

23. CONCAVE ROPE. Pipe spring-shape in clockwise direction, using even pressure and keeping bag horizontal.

24. Continue piping to form the curve shown. Stop piping and pull bag away in a half-turn.

25. SPIRAL SHELL. Hold piping bag at the angle shown and start to press.

26. Continue piping in clockwise direction, increasing the size of the circle with each turn.

27. Continue piping in clockwise direction but, from the centre, decrease the size of the circle with each turn.

28. To complete spiral shell, stop piping and pull bag away in a half-turn.

29. 'C' SCROLL. Pipe in clockwise direction, increasing the size of the circle to form the body.

30. Continue piping, reducing the size of the circles, then form the tail – using reduced pressure.

31. REVERSE 'C' SCROLL. Pipe in a clockwise direction, increasing the size of the circle to form the body.

32. Continue piping, reducing the size of the circles, then form the tail – using reduced pressure.

33. 'S' SCROLL. Hold piping bag at angle shown and start to press.

34. Continue piping in a clockwise direction, increasing the size of each circle to form the body.

35. Continue piping, reducing the size of the circles from the centre.

36. Continue piping and form the tail by reducing pressure.

37. REVERSED 'S' SCROLL. Hold piping bag at angle shown and start to press.

38. Continue piping in an anti-clockwise direction, increasing the size of each circle to form the body.

39. Continue piping, reducing the size of the circles from the centre.

40. Continue piping and form the tail by reducing pressure.

Before attempting to pipe any one shape, please study the whole sequence of photographs and notes for that shape.

(using either royal icing or buttercream)

By following the touch, lift and drop instructions (page 40), many different styles of writing can be achieved. However, it may be advisable to continually practice and use one writing style only. This design is, perhaps, the most suitable for practice.

Piping – Tube Shapes and Uses

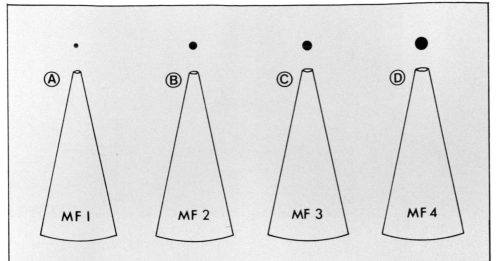

PLAIN TUBES

Plain tubes are used for piping lattice, filigree, writing, small piped designs and overpiping.

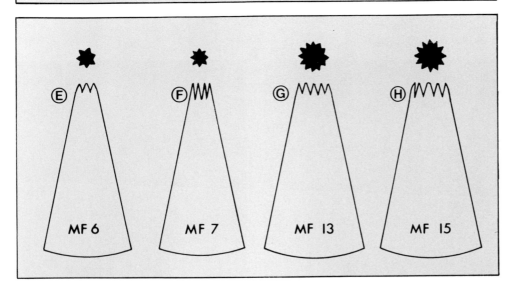

COARSE STAR TUBES

Coarse Star tubes are used for piped shapes (as on pages 38 and 39) where deep definition in the piped shape is required.

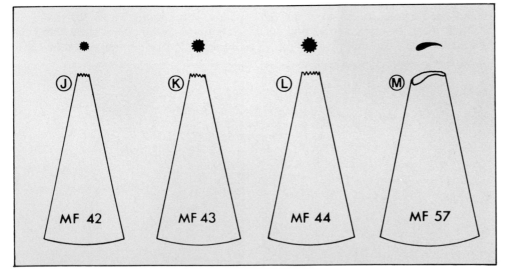

FINE STAR TUBES

Fine Star tubes are used for piped shapes where shallow definition is required. This allows for overpiping the piped shape (as on page 64).

Petal tubes are used for piping flowers (as on page 50).

As manufacturers allocate different reference numbers to their respective icing tubes, it is necessary to match the shape of the tube tip required with one of these illustrations AND NOT TO TRY AND MATCH A NUMBER (unless it is a Mary Ford tube).

Tubes used in piped work within this book are identified by the following symbols –

Ⓐ   Ⓑ   Ⓒ   Ⓓ..........

and these form part of the respective step-by-step instructions.

(NOTE: The 'MF' followed by a number on each of these tubes are the Mary Ford manufactured tube reference numbers).

Creating Round Cake-Top Paper Templates

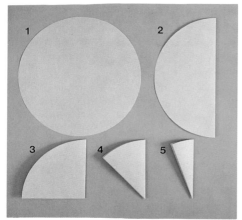

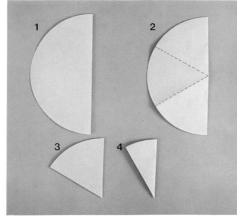

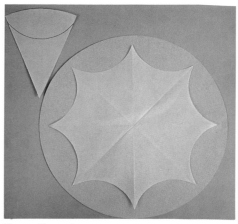

A. To form 2, 4, 8, or 16 sections.
Cut paper to fit cake-top (1).
Fold (1) = (2) – 2 sections.
Fold (2) = (3) – 4 sections.
Fold (3) = (4) – 8 sections.
Fold (4) = (5) – 16 sections.

B. To form 2, 6 or 12 sections.
Cut paper to fit cake-top.
Fold = (1) – 2 sections.
Mark (1) into 3 equal sections = (2).
Fold (2) = (3) – 6 sections.
Fold (3) = (4) – 12 sections.

C. = 8 sections.
Follow instructions in 'A' to make 8 sections. Mark the curve shown and cut. Unfold and place centrally on cake top.

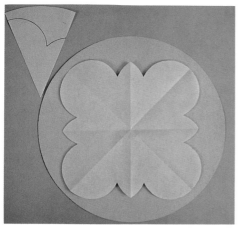

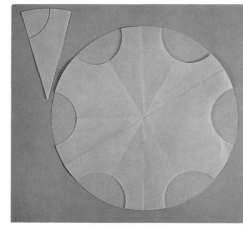

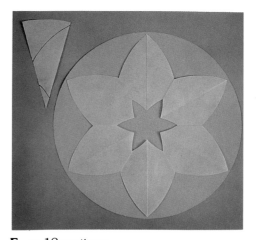

D. = 8 sections.
Follow instructions in 'A' to make 8 sections. Mark the curves shown and cut. Unfold and place centrally on cake-top.

E. = 12 sections.
Follow instructions in 'B' to make 12 sections. Mark the curve shown and cut. Unfold and place centrally on cake-top.

F. = 12 sections.
Follow instructions in 'B' to make 12 sections. Mark the curves shown and cut. Unfold and place centrally on cake-top.

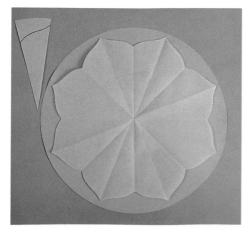

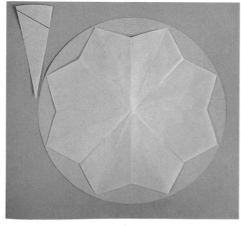

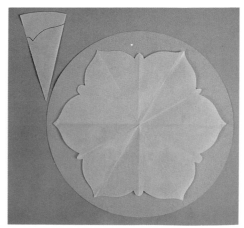

G. = 12 sections.
Following instructions in 'B' to make 12 sections. Mark the curves shown and cut. Unfold and place centrally on cake-top.

H. = 16 sections.
Follow instructions in 'A' to make 16 sections. Mark the line shown and cut. Unfold and place centrally on cake-top.

I. = 16 sections.
Follow instructions in 'A' to make 16 sections. Mark the curve shown and cut. Unfold and place centrally on cake-top.

Creating Square Cake-Top Paper Templates

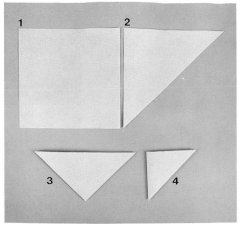

A. Cut paper to fit cake-top.
Fold (1) diagonally = (2).
Fold (2) in half = (3).
Fold (3) in half = (4).

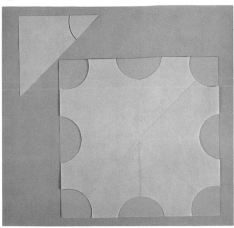

B. Follow whole sequence in A. Mark the curve shown and cut. Unfold and place centrally on cake-top.

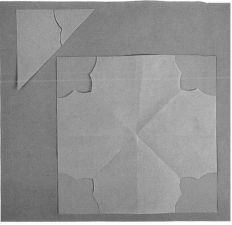

C. Follow whole sequence in A. Mark the curve shown and cut. Unfold and place centrally on cake-top.

D. Follow whole sequence in A. Mark the curve shown and cut. Unfold and place centrally on cake-top.

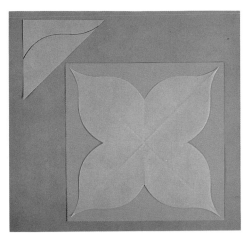

E. Follow whole sequence in A. Mark the curve shown and cut. Unfold and place centrally on cake-top.

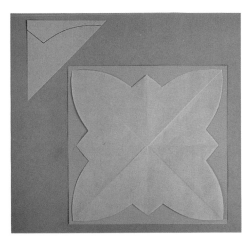

F. Follow whole sequence in A. Mark the curve shown and cut. Unfold and place centrally on cake-top.

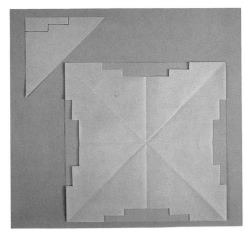

G. Follow whole sequence in A. Mark the line shown and cut. Unfold and place centrally on cake-top.

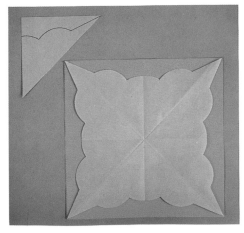

H. Follow whole sequence in A. Mark the lines shown and cut. Unfold and place centrally on cake-top.

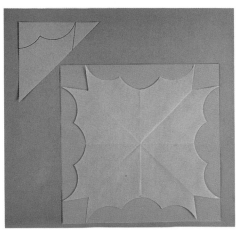

I. Follow whole sequence in A. Mark the line and curves shown and cut. Unfold and place centrally on cake-top.

MAKING A RUNOUT

1. Make royal icing 24 hours before use. Colour as required.

2. Add and stir in water to sufficient royal icing for the runout filling.

3. Continue adding and mixing water until it reaches a dropping consistency.

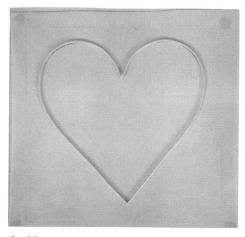

4. Draw the required design (template) on paper and then secure it on a tile or flat surface.

5. Overlay the template with a piece of waxed paper and secure.

6. Using the royal icing set aside for outlining and decorating, pipe a line over the template line.   Ⓐ

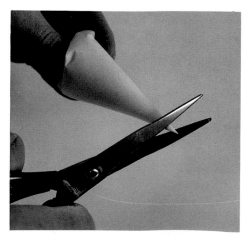

7. Fill a piping bag with the royal icing runout filling and cut a small tip off end.

8. Fill the outline by starting to pipe at the top and then by working from side to side down towards the bottom.

9. Keeping an even thickness completely fill the outline. Leave to dry 24 hours in a warm dry place. Decorate as required.

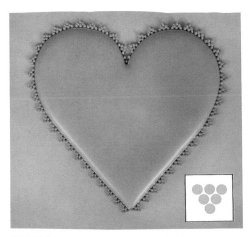

DECORATING A RUNOUT
1. Pipe small dots around the edge of a dried runout.   Ⓐ

2. Pipe motif of choice and decorate runout. Leave to dry for 12 hours in a dry warm place.   Ⓐ

3. Carefully pull waxed paper over a table's edge to release runout. Note: Place a cloth under the runout in case it falls.

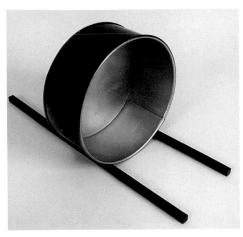

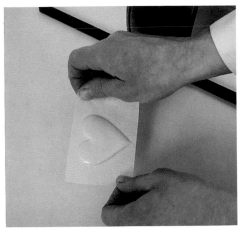

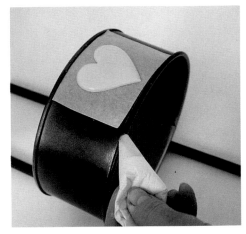

MAKING A CURVED RUNOUT
1. Fix the tin (used to bake the cake) in an upright position.

2. Now follow steps 1-9 on page 46 but on completion of filling, lift the runout from template.

3. *Immediately* place and fix the runout over the top of the cake-tin, as shown. Leave to dry for 24 hours in a warm dry place. Decorate as required.

MAKING A LARGE RUNOUT COLLAR
1. Follow steps 1-7 on page 46. Start to fill the collar outline, as shown.

2. Continue filling by adding icing at each end (to avoid crusting), until the collar is completely filled.

3. Cut a 1″ cross in waxed paper's centre. Leave to dry for 24 hours in a warm dry place. Decorate as required.

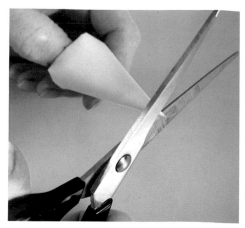

FIGURE PIPING

1. Use royal icing made 24 hours before. Place in bowl and soften with a drop of cold water.

2. Colour small amounts of royal icing by mixing on a tile with palette knife.

3. Make sufficient small piping bags for the required colours then fill each with a different colour. Cut a small tip off each bag.

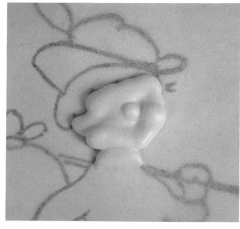

4. Draw the required design (template) on paper, secure on a tile or flat surface, then overlay and fix waxed paper.

5. Pipe-in face, ensuring that the cheeks and nose are thicker and eyes more shallow. Then pipe-in the neck.

6. Pipe-in the stick, hat, boots and legs in the appropriate colours.

7. Pipe-in shorts, bag, gloves, boot tops and hair with appropriate colours.

8. Complete the figure by piping the sweater and feather in the appropriate colours. Leave to dry 24 hours in a warm dry place.

9. Paint the face and other features shown (using edible food colourings). See page 47, No.3. to remove figure from waxed paper.

(Using royal icing without glycerine.)

PIPED FLOWERS
1. Fix waxed paper to top of flower nail.

2. Turn nail whilst piping through a petal tube to form each petal. When complete, leave to dry for 12 hours. Ⓜ

PIPED LEAVES
1. Mark, then cut tip off filled piping bag where indicated.

2. Pipe leaf to required size.

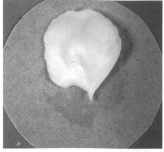   

SEQUENCE SHOWING BASIC FLOWER CONSTRUCTION

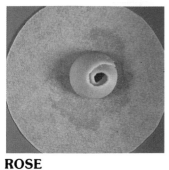 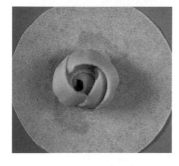  

ROSE

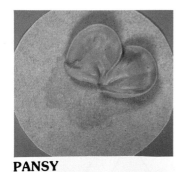 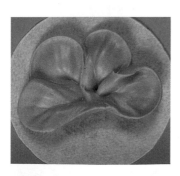  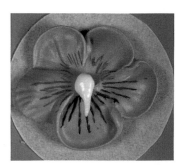

PANSY

 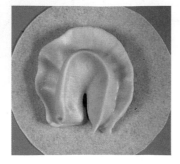  

SWEET PEA

ROSE
1. Roll sugar paste to form a cone.

2. Shape first petal from further sugar paste.

3. Remove surplus sugar paste from petal. Dampen with water and fix around cone.

4. Make and fix second petal opposite first petal.

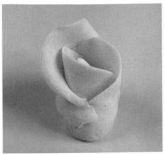

5. Make and fix third petal, then curl petal edge.

6. Make and fix fourth petal, then curl petal edge.

7. Make and fix fifth petal, then curl petal edge.

8. Make and fix additional petals to required size.

CARNATION
1. Roll out and cut a fluted disc of sugar paste.

2. Fold in half after rolling each flute with a cocktail stick.

3. Gather edges to form flower's centre. Repeat 1-3 and fix together.

4. Repeat 1-3 as necessary to form full bloom, then shade petal edges to colours required.

BASIC FLOWER
1. Roll out a sugar paste cone and push it on to a pencil shaped stick.

2. Cut six slits in the cone, as indicated.

3. Remove sugar paste and, with finger and thumb, press out each section to a petal shape.

4. Shade inside the flower to colour required, then pipe centre.

1. Prepare a buttercream coated sponge using a serrated scraper around the side. Then cover lower cake-side with roasted flaked almonds.

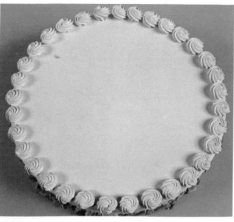

2. Pipe rosettes around cake-top edge with buttercream. Ⓕ

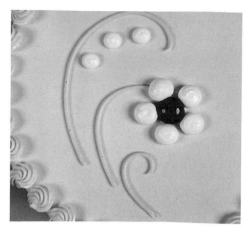

3. Pipe lines and bulbs with buttercream to create a floral spray and finish with half a cherry. Ⓒ

4. Pipe the vertical wavy line and dots with buttercream. Then fix jelly diamonds to represent leaves. Ⓑ

5. Pipe name of choice to the right of the wavy line with buttercream. Ⓑ

Bold and dramatic piping quickly produces a floral design to suit any gateaux.

Before commencing any work on this page, please read the whole sequence of instructions and ensure you have the proper equipment and materials, as well as sufficient time to complete the project. Additional information can be found on pages 6-51 (Index on pages 94-95).

1. Coat a square sponge with buttercream and then cover the bottom half of each cake-side with vermicelli.

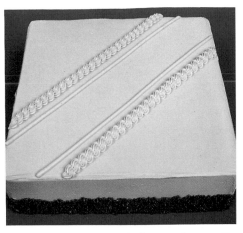

2. Pipe ropes and lines diagonally across the cake-top with buttercream. Ⓕ Ⓒ

3. Pipe inscription of choice between the lines and then overpipe lines in a strong colour with buttercream. Ⓑ

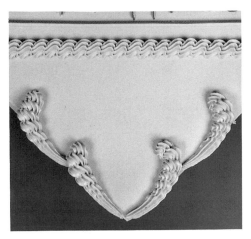

4. Pipe 'C' scrolls on opposite corners, as shown with buttercream. Ⓕ

5. Pipe shells and a rosette within the corner 'C' scrolls with buttercream. Ⓕ

Add coffee beans to complete the cake-top.

This cake gives the appearance of being different from other square cakes because of the corner-to-corner piping.

Before commencing any work on this page, please read the whole sequence of instructions and ensure you have the proper equipment and materials, as well as sufficient time to complete the project. Additional information can be found on pages 6-51 (Index on pages 94-95).

1. Cut and fix a sugarpaste band over a sugar-pasted sponge cake.

2. Pipe lines beside the band and around the cake-top edge with royal icing, as shown. Ⓐ

3. Pipe the further curved lines shown. Ⓐ

4. Pipe flowers at the end of each curved line and then pipe stems and leaves, as shown. Ⓐ

5. Pipe inscription of choice on the band. Ⓐ Ⓑ

This design is bound to please the 'Grandma' age group and can be adapted to incorporate her favourite colours.

Before commencing any work on this page, please read the whole sequence of instructions and ensure you have the proper equipment and materials, as well as sufficient time to complete the project. Additional information can be found on pages 6-51 (Index on pages 94-95).

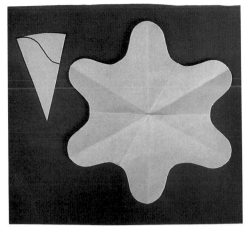

1. Follow instructions on page 44-B and then draw and cut the curved line in the shape shown, to form template.

2. Place template on top of sugar-pasted sponge cake and pipe a line around the edge of the template with royal icing. Leave for 10 minutes and then remove template. Ⓐ

3. Pipe the floral design shown. Ⓐ Ⓑ

4. Pipe further leaf and stem design. Ⓐ

5. Fix ribbon around cake-base and then pipe curved lines around cake-side. Ⓐ

This embroidery style design would grace any ladies coffee morning or afternoon tea party table.

Before commencing any work on this page, please read the whole sequence of instructions and ensure you have the proper equipment and materials, as well as sufficient time to complete the project. Additional information can be found on pages 6-51 (Index on pages 94-95).

1. Thinly coat a filled sponge with buttercream. Then roll out sufficient sugar paste to cover the sponge top and sides.

2. Carefully place the sugar paste over the sponge, ensuring there are no trapped air pockets on the cake top.

3. Gently ease sugar paste into the cake sides with the hand (without creasing the sugar paste).

4. Trim surplus sugar paste from cake base. Then remove air pockets by pricking with a pin.

5. Using a cake-smoother, polish the top and sides to give a flat even surface. Leave to crust over.

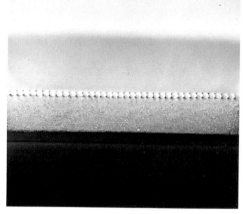

6. Pipe plain shells around cake-base with royal icing. Ⓑ

7. Mark each side of the cake (with a sharp pointed instrument) into three equal curves, using a cut card as a guide.

8. Roll out and cut with cake cutters, a thin sheet of sugar paste to the shape shown.

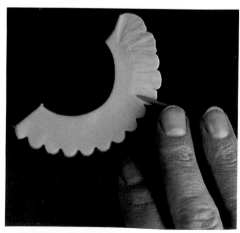

9. Roll a cocktail stick backwards and forwards over the fluted edge to create a Garrett frill.

Before commencing any work on this page, please read the whole sequence of instructions and ensure you have the proper equipment and materials, as well as sufficient time to complete the project. Additional information can be found on pages 6-51 (Index on pages 94-95).

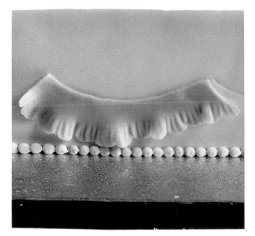

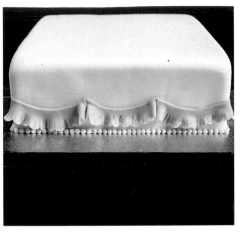

10. Brush a thin water line below a marked cake-side line. Then fix frill and trim to size. Lift out frill base to give effect shown.

11. Repeat 8-10 to complete one side, ensuring frill ends are neatly joined.

12. Fix frills along each remaining cake-side. Lift out corners to give a flare effect.

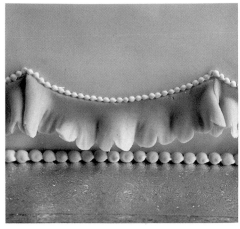

13. Pipe small shells along upper curve of each frill. Ⓒ

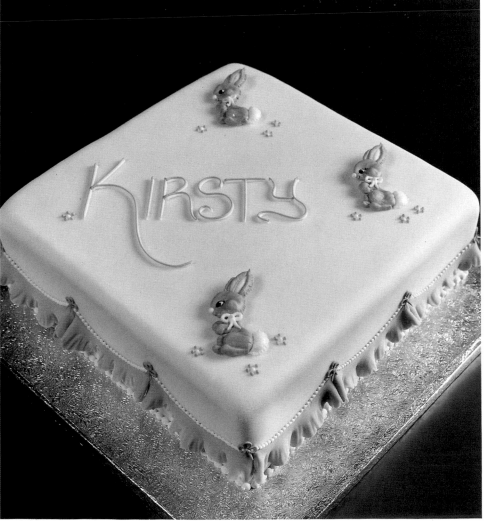

14. Pipe a small bow at the top of each curve. Ⓒ

Pipe inscription of choice and fix runout rabbits to cake top and surround with piped flowers. Ⓒ

Sugar paste and royal icing combines to make this a delicate christening or youngster's birthday theme.

Before commencing any work on this page, please read the whole sequence of instructions and ensure you have the proper equipment and materials, as well as sufficient time to complete the project. Additional information can be found on pages 6-51 (Index on pages 94-95).

1. Cut top corners off square sponge, as shown.

2. Position cut pieces at top to form roof of bird-box.

3. Partially mix edible colouring into sugar paste to give woodgrain effect.

4. Jam and cream sponge and cover with the sugar paste. Place on coated board in position shown.

5. Cut and fix coloured sugar paste pieces to form eaves, hole and perch.

6. Use royal icing to pipe branches, then stroke with a brush to create bark effect.

7. Cut and fix sugar paste leaves to branches.

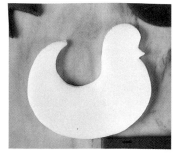

8. Cut and fix sugar paste dove to perch.

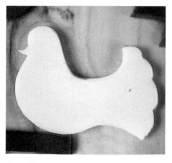

9. Cut and fix another sugar paste dove to the perch.

10. Use royal icing to pipe dove features.　Ⓐ

11. Cut and fix a sugar paste heart to the cake-board.

12. Pipe message of choice on the heart.　Ⓑ

Love, symbolised by the white doves, is the theme of this cake and is, therefore, ideal for Valentine's Day, an Engagement or Mother's Day.

Before commencing any work on this page, please read the whole sequence of instructions and ensure you have the proper equipment and materials, as well as sufficient time to complete the project. Additional information can be found on pages 6-51 (Index on pages 94-95).

1. Two square sponges required. Cut top corners off one sponge, as shown. Position cut pieces to form sentry box roof.

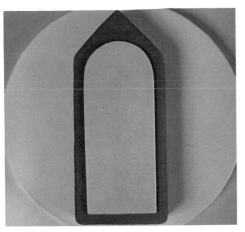

2. Jam and cream sponge. Cover in sugar paste. Place on coated board and then cut and fix sugar paste sentry box front.

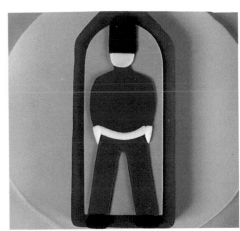

3. Cut and fix sugar paste shapes shown to form the sentry.

4. Decorate the sentry, as shown with royal icing. Ⓐ

5. Pipe inscription of choice on cakeboard. Ⓐ Ⓑ

Simple piped lines complete this cake by forming both ground and sky. A cake to delight every boy – who will be the envy of his friends. Ⓐ

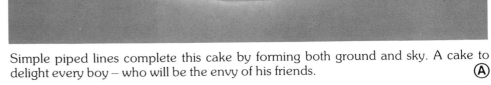

Before commencing any work on this page, please read the whole sequence of instructions and ensure you have the proper equipment and materials, as well as sufficient time to complete the project. Additional information can be found on pages 6-51 (Index on pages 94-95).

1. Cut large sponge in the shape shown to hold small sponge.

2. Divide off-cut into four equal parts to form wings and feet.

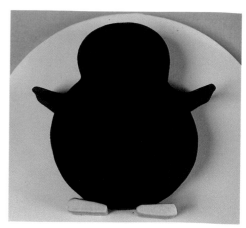

3. Jam and cream sponge and cover with sugar paste. Place on coated board in position shown.

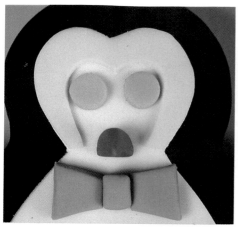

4. Cut and fix sugar paste pieces to form face and bow-tie.

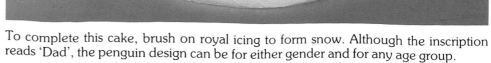

5. Decorate face with piped royal icing and then pipe inscription of choice. Ⓐ

To complete this cake, brush on royal icing to form snow. Although the inscription reads 'Dad', the penguin design can be for either gender and for any age group.

Before commencing any work on this page, please read the whole sequence of instructions and ensure you have the proper equipment and materials, as well as sufficient time to complete the project. Additional information can be found on pages 6-51 (Index on pages 94-95).

1. Cover a square sponge top with sugar paste. Then coat sides with roasted nibbed almonds.

2. Roll out, cut and fix sugar paste sea and hull.

3. Roll out, cut and fix sugar paste sails.

4. Pipe masts, port holes, ship's decoration (piped shells) and sea waves, with royal icing. Then make and fix sugar paste flags. Ⓒ Ⓙ

5. Pipe curved lines to form clouds. Then pipe inscription of choice on sails. Mark sails with brush lines. Ⓐ Ⓑ

An excellent design for the adventurous boy and one which is within every cake decorator's capability. Ⓕ

Before commencing any work on this page, please read the whole sequence of instructions and ensure you have the proper equipment and materials, as well as sufficient time to complete the project. Additional information can be found on pages 6-51 (Index on pages 94-95).

Using piped royal icing

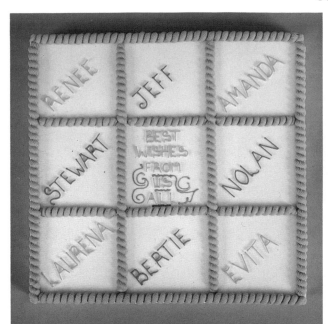

Ⓐ
Ⓑ
Ⓚ

This cake displays, in piped icing, the names of the participants in any grand celebration.

This neat design is eminently suitable for the 'coming-of-age' celebratory party, whether it be for the 18 or 21 year old.

Ⓐ Ⓑ Ⓔ

Ⓐ Ⓑ Ⓕ

A cake for the sportsman which can be adapted for any sport and age. This design illustrates a cricketing theme for the octogenarian.

Practised scroll-work should enable any cake decorator to produce this 'any occasion' formal and effective feminine design.

Ⓐ
Ⓑ
Ⓒ
Ⓛ

Using piped royal icing

Ella's birthday cake illustrates the use of large piped lettering and simple piped Reverse Skein bordering.

Ⓐ Ⓑ Ⓖ

Artificial decorations and accurate piping are the predominant characteristics of this friendly round cake.

Ⓐ Ⓑ Ⓒ Ⓙ

Ⓐ Ⓑ Ⓓ

Hippoty and Hoppity heartily hop across meadows and hillocks to hail Harry's happy second birthday.

Ⓐ
Ⓑ
Ⓚ

A combed scraper and two colours present the basic background to this nautical theme. The seascape is emphasised with plunging anchors.

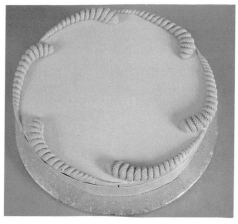

1. Marzipan (Page 26) and coat the top of a cake (Pages 30-31 No's. 8-11). Then pipe 'C' scrolls around top edge with royal icing, as shown. Ⓛ

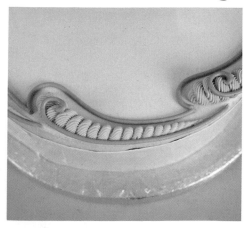

2. Pipe a line inside each 'C' scroll and then pipe a line on top of each 'C' scroll. Ⓒ

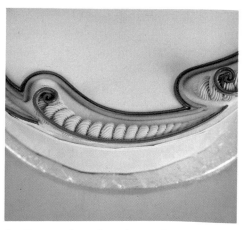

3. Pipe a line beside each inside line and then overpipe each top line. Ⓑ

4. Pipe inscription of choice and then decorate the first letter in the manner shown. Ⓐ Ⓑ

5. Decorate second letter in the manner shown. Ⓐ

Complete the decoration by adding artificial flowers and leaves of choice and by fixing ribbon to cake-side.

A dignified cake produced by cleanly piped lines and inscription.

Before commencing any work on this page, please read the whole sequence of instructions and ensure you have the proper equipment and materials, as well as sufficient time to complete the project. Additional information can be found on pages 6-51 (Index on pages 94-95).

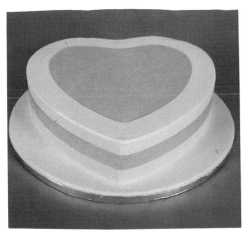 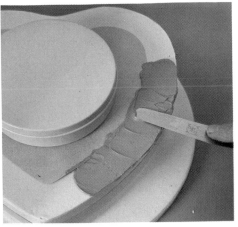 

1. Cut a piece of card for the cake top in the proportion shown. Then cut a card band for the cake-side.

2. Hold down cake-top card with a weight. Thinly spread royal icing around the top rim of the cake.

3. Immediately stipple royal icing by dabbing it with a dry sponge.

4. Repeat No.'s 2-3 on cake-side and cake-board and then remove cards from cake-top and side. Leave to dry 1 hour.

5. Pipe bulbs on inside of cake-top rim, around cake-top edge and around cake base. Ⓒ Ⓓ

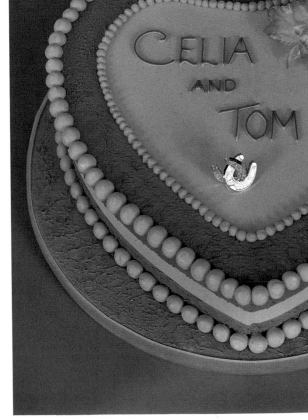

Pipe inscription of choice and fix artificial decorations to cake-top and ribbon around cake-board. Ⓐ Ⓑ

Note: Where time is of the essence, this style of decoration will please.

Before commencing any work on this page, please read the whole sequence of instructions and ensure you have the proper equipment and materials, as well as sufficient time to complete the project. Additional information can be found on pages 6-51 (Index on pages 94-95).

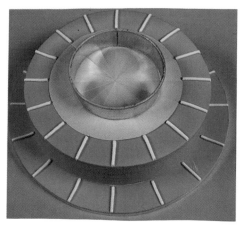

1. Weigh down a paper disc on cake-top. Pipe lines on cake-top and board with royal icing to form 16 equal divisions on each. Ⓒ

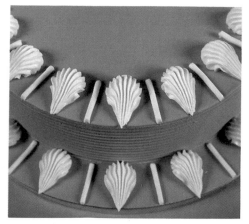

2. Remove paper disc and pipe a shell at each division. Ⓖ

3. Pipe inscription of choice on cake-top. Ⓑ

4. Overpipe inscription and each piped dividing line. Ⓐ

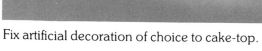

5. Pipe a dot each side of each shell. Ⓒ

Fix artificial decoration of choice to cake-top.

Limited piping skills can, with a little practice, produce this colourful professional cake design.

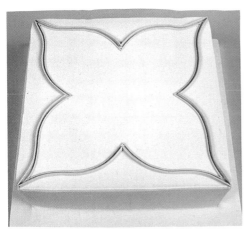

1. Template 'E' on page 45 is required. Outline template with piped royal icing lines, as shown. Remove template.
Ⓑ Ⓒ

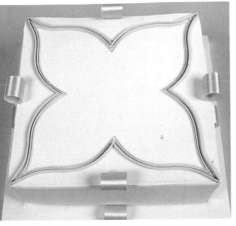

2. Roll and fix satin ribbon to cake-top edge, as shown and then to the centre of each cake-side base.

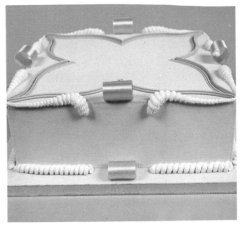

3. Pipe an 'S' scroll to each cake-top corner and a rope to each cake-base corner. Finish each corner with a piped rosette.
Ⓛ

4. Pipe inscription of choice on cake-top and then fix an appropriate artificial decoration of choice. .
Ⓐ Ⓑ

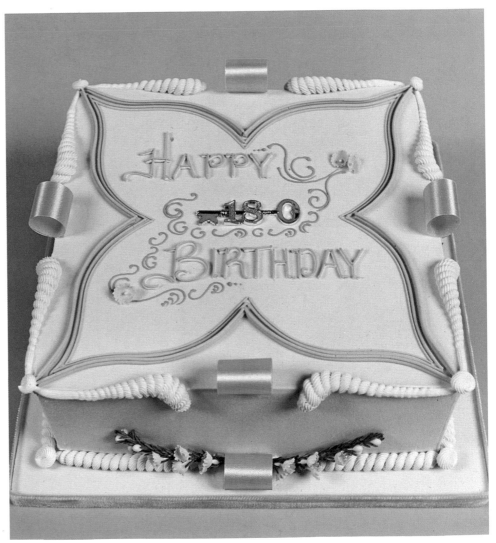

5. Decorate inscription with piped tracery and artificial flowers.
Ⓐ

Fix artificial flowers to cake-base and ribbon around cake-board.

This cake proves that a beautiful pattern can be achieved by piping large curved lines in a formal design.

Before commencing any work on this page, please read the whole sequence of instructions and ensure you have the proper equipment and materials, as well as sufficient time to complete the project. Additional information can be found on pages 6-51 (Index on pages 94-95).

67

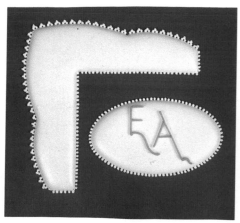

1. Make and decorate cake-top corner and cake-side runouts (with royal icing) to appropriate proportions (See pages 46, 47 and 49). Ⓐ

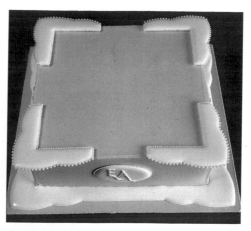

2. Outline and flood-in cake-board to a matching pattern. Fix corner and cake-side runouts. Leave to dry 12 hours. Ⓑ

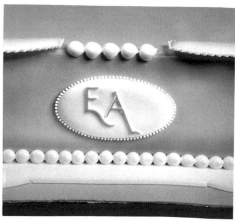

3. Pipe plain shells around cake-base and between cake-top runouts. Ⓒ

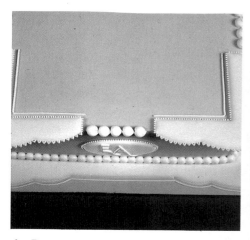

4. Pipe a line inside each cake-top runout and beside each cake-board runout. Ⓑ

5. Pipe and decorate inscription of choice on cake-top. Ⓐ

Complete the cake-top by fixing doves to the inscription and the cake-base by adding artificial flowers and leaves to each corner.

This cake is for the more skilled craftsman, who has to properly plan and execute the balance of the design.

Before commencing any work on this page, please read the whole sequence of instructions and ensure you have the proper equipment and materials, as well as sufficient time to complete the project. Additional information can be found on pages 6-51 (Index on pages 94-95).

68

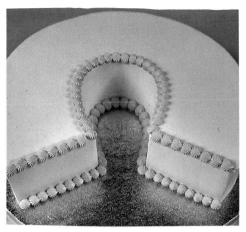

1. Pipe shells around the part of the cake-base and cake-top shown with royal icing. (L)

2. Pipe spiral shells around the outside curve of the cake-base and the cake-top edge. (L)

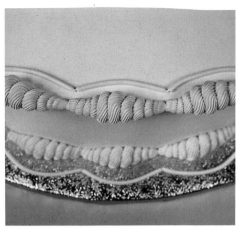

3. Pipe curved lines on the cake-board and the cake-top, as shown. (C)

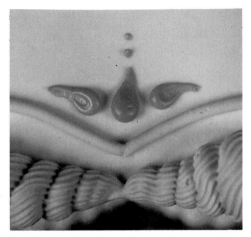

4. Pipe a floral motif at each curved line join. (B)

5. Pipe graduated dots between each cake-top shell. (A)

A piped inscription and artificial decorations complete the top of this cake. (A) (B)

The horseshoe is a symbol of good luck, both for the present and the future and, therefore, will always please the lucky recipient.

1. Cover cake-top and side with coloured almond paste/marzipan.

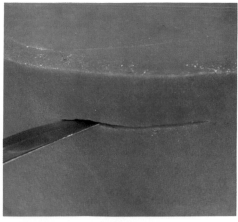

2. Cut a line 2″ long through the depth of the cake-side almond paste/marzipan.

3. Form a pocket by easing the almond paste/marzipan away from the side of the cake. Repeat No's. 2 and 3 around cake-side.

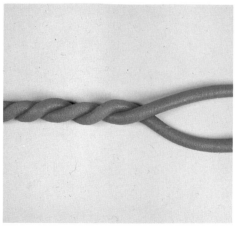

4. Roll out and intertwine two lengths of almond paste/marzipan to form cake borders.

5. Fix borders to cake-top and cake-base.

6. Press coloured almond paste/marzipan through a wire sieve to create 'plant growth'.

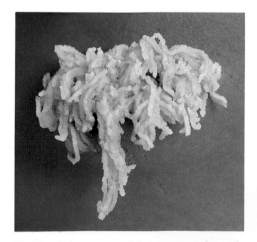

7. Fix 'plant growth' into a cake-side pocket.

8. Repeat No's. 6 and 7 to fill each pocket.

9. Press different colours of almond paste/marzipan through a wire sieve and fix to 'plant growth' to give floral effect.

Before commencing any work on this page, please read the whole sequence of instructions and ensure you have the proper equipment and materials, as well as sufficient time to complete the project. Additional information can be found on pages 6-51 (Index on pages 94-95).

10. Press coloured almond paste/ marzipan through a wire sieve to create mossy earth for cake-top.

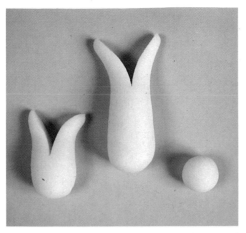

11. Roll out and cut almond paste/ marzipan to form rabbit parts, as shown. (5 rabbits required).

12. Fix rabbit parts together and pipe in face details with royal icing. Ⓐ

13. Cut out a sugar paste/marzipan sign-stone and decorate with piped message of choice. Ⓐ

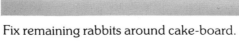

14. Fix two rabbits and sign-stone to cake-top.

Fix remaining rabbits around cake-board.

This cake indicates the versatility of modelling with almond paste/marzipan to a person with a creative mind. An ideal cake for marzipan lovers.

Before commencing any work on this page, please read the whole sequence of instructions and ensure you have the proper equipment and materials, as well as sufficient time to complete the project. Additional information can be found on pages 6-51 (Index on pages 94-95).

Note: Mix 3 tablespoons of royal icing with ¼ teaspoon of clear piping jelly for all brushed royal icing work.

1. Draw and cut out paper templates. Place on coated cake-top and scratch template outlines into the cake-top. Then remove the templates.

2. Overpipe a petal scratch line with royal icing and immediately brush the icing to the centre of the petal. Ⓒ

3. Repeat for each petal and then pipe dots to form flower centre. Ⓐ Ⓒ

4. Repeat No.2 for each leaf and then pipe leaf veins. Ⓐ Ⓒ

5. Pipe stems. Ⓑ

Complete cake by piping – scrolls and shells along cake-top edges; shells around cake base; inscription of choice and decorative cake-board edge. Fix ribbon around cake-side. Ⓐ Ⓚ

This style of decoration is an ideal medium for the natural artist.

Before commencing any work on this page, please read the whole sequence of instructions and ensure you have the proper equipment and materials, as well as sufficient time to complete the project. Additional information can be found on pages 6-51 (Index on pages 94-95).

1. Template 'F' on page 44 required. Outline template with piped royal icing lines, as shown and pipe graduated bulbs round cake-base. Remove template. Ⓒ

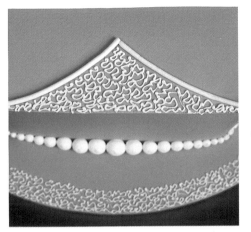

2. Pipe filigree into each cake-top section, as indicated, then around cake-board edge. Ⓐ

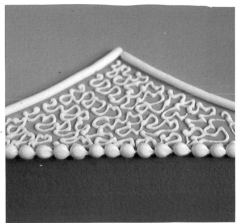

3. Pipe plain shells around cake-top edge. Ⓑ

4. Pipe lily-of-the-valley floral motif on each cake-side. Ⓐ

5. Fix previously made runout (see pages 46 and 49) butterflies to each cake-top corner.

Finish the artwork by fixing an artificial rose and leaves to the cake-top centre and a horseshoe to each cake-base corner. An ideal cake for the lover of nature's flora and fauna.

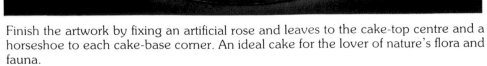

Before commencing any work on this page, please read the whole sequence of instructions and ensure you have the proper equipment and materials, as well as sufficient time to complete the project. Additional information can be found on pages 6-51 (Index on pages 94-95).

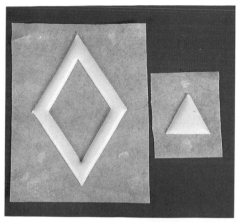

1. Outline and flood-in (with royal icing) 8 triangles for each cake-side and 4 diamonds. Leave to dry for 24 hours. Ⓐ

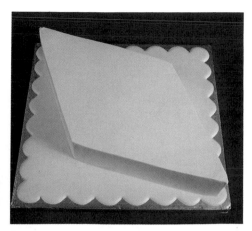

2. Place coated cake in position shown, then outline and flood-in cake-board. Leave to dry for 24 hours. Ⓑ

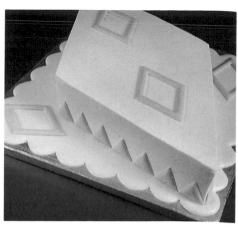

3. Fix diamond and triangle runouts in positions shown.

4. Pipe shells around cake-top edge with royal icing. Ⓚ

5. Pipe inscription of choice across cake-top and embellish with piped tracery. Ⓐ Ⓑ

Fix artificial flowers and leaves to each diamond runout and corner.

A cluster of edible diamonds ideally suits the celebration of any Diamond Wedding Anniversary (60 years).

74

Before commencing any work on this page, please read the whole sequence of instructions and ensure you have the proper equipment and materials, as well as sufficient time to complete the project. Additional information can be found on pages 6-51 (Index on pages 94-95).

1. Twist and fix a sugar paste candle and flame, then roll out, cut and fix an open sugar paste card.

2. Pipe inscription of choice on to the card with royal icing. Ⓐ

3. Pipe the small leaf design shown, then fix sugar paste ivy leaves to base of candle. Ⓐ

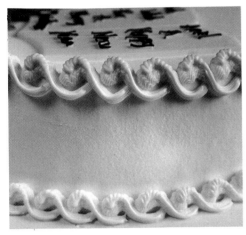

4. Pipe 'S' scrolls around half the cake-top edge and around the cake base. Then overpipe each 'S' scroll. Ⓑ Ⓚ

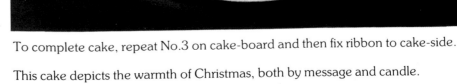

5. Overpipe each 'S' scroll and then pipe candle flame lines. Ⓐ

To complete cake, repeat No.3 on cake-board and then fix ribbon to cake-side. Ⓐ

This cake depicts the warmth of Christmas, both by message and candle.

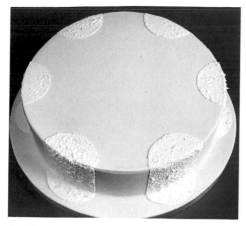

1. Follow instructions on page 44-E and place template on cake-top. Then stipple each panel with royal icing, as shown. Remove template.

2. Pipe shells between each panel at cake-top edge and base. Ⓚ

3. Make and fix sugar paste holly leaves to each panel, as shown, then complete holly spray with piped berries.

4. Pipe message of choice on cake-top. Ⓐ Ⓑ

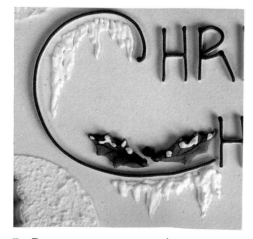

5. Decorate inscription with sugar paste holly leaves and piped berries, then pipe icicles. Ⓐ

Underline the inscription with a piped decorative line; fix sugar bells; then pipe a dot between each shell. Ⓐ

The snow and icicles on this cake represent traditional Christmas English weather.

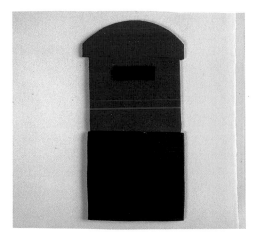

1. Roll out, cut and fix sugar paste pieces to form a letter box.

2. Decorate the letter box and then 'cover' ground, middle and top of letter box with piped (royal icing) snow. Ⓐ

3. Pipe tree branches, then decorate with a runout robin with letter and then piped snow. Ⓑ

4. Pipe inscription of choice and falling snow. Ⓐ Ⓑ

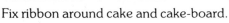

5. Pipe 'S' and 'C' scrolls and shells around cake-top edge, then pipe 'snow' around cake-base, as shown. Ⓕ

Fix ribbon around cake and cake-board.

The robin with a letter symbolises this season of goodwill wishes to all.

Before commencing any work on this page, please read the whole sequence of instructions and ensure you have the proper equipment and materials, as well as sufficient time to complete the project. Additional information can be found on pages 6-51 (Index on pages 94-95).

Wedding Cake Guidelines

1. Only use a well tried quality recipe for the cake(s).

* * *

2. During the maturing period, do not add too much alcohol to the cake (as this may work through the marzipan and discolour the icing or sugar paste).

* * *

3. Plan well ahead –
 (a) When preparing the cake mixture, ensure there is sufficient for the number of tiers required and the size of each tier.
 (b) The cake(s) should be made at least 8 weeks before the wedding.
 (c) Marzipan the cake(s) four weeks before the wedding.
 (d) Complete coating and decorating the cake(s) one week before the wedding.
 (e) On average, each pound of decorated wedding cake will serve six–eight people. In cases where a large distribution of wedding cake is required, separate slabs of coated cake can be cut at the wedding for this purpose.
 (f) Should the top tier need to be a sponge cake, use the genoese recipe on page 8 and make it ten days before the wedding. Marzipan and decorate within four days of the wedding. (Note: If using royal icing to coat the genoese top tier, mix three teaspoons of glycerine into each pound of royal icing being used).

* * *

4. A well balanced multi-tier cake should consist of cakes of matching depth.

* * *

5. To ensure stability of a multi-tiered cake, strictly follow the glycerine table on page 15.

* * *

6. Although it is usual to see a white cake as the centre-piece of a wedding reception, discreet colours can be used to match the general colour theme (e.g. the bridesmaids flowers and/or dresses).

* * *

7. The completed wedding cake should be kept in cardboard boxes in a dry warm atmosphere and away from direct sunlight.

* * *

8. Do not attempt to tier the cake until the wedding day reception.

* * *

9. A wedding cake should be transported with each tier in a separate box, either in the boot or on the floor of the car (DO NOT place on seats).

* * *

10. Unless the bottom tier has a wedge (see opposite page), it will be necessary for the bride and groom to use a strong sharp knife to make the first (ceremonial) cut.

11. The easiest way to obtain nicely sized portions, is to –
 (a) cut the cake in half with a strong, *sharp*, scalloped large knife which has been dipped in hot water;
 (b) place half the cake on to a clean cutting board;
 (c) divide the top into equal portions by marking it with a sharp knife;
 (d) cut a complete slice from the inside side of the cake;
 (e) lay the slice flat and then cut it into the marked portions; then repeat process, as necessary.
 (f) keep the knife clean by occasionally dipping it in hot water and then wiping it with a damp cloth.

* * *

12. Always cut a genoese sponge cake with a dampened knife.

* * *

13. Storage –
 (a) Decorated genoese sponge wedding cake should not be stored.
 (b) A cut fruit cake should be sealed in waxed paper and stored in a cardboard box in a cool, *dry* atmosphere.
 (c) An uncut fruit cake should be stored in a cardboard box in a cool, *dry* atmosphere.

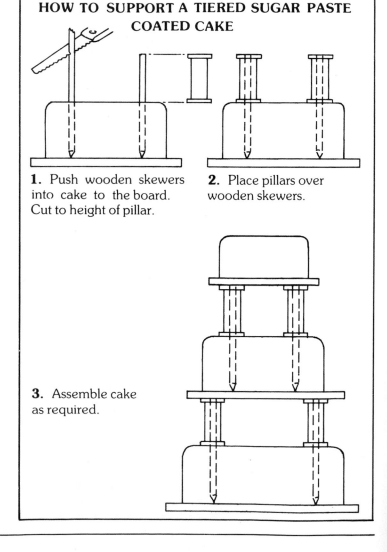

HOW TO SUPPORT A TIERED SUGAR PASTE COATED CAKE

1. Push wooden skewers into cake to the board. Cut to height of pillar.

2. Place pillars over wooden skewers.

3. Assemble cake as required.

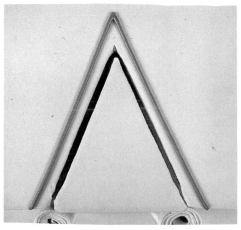

1. Pipe a line beside the cut wedge with royal icing. **Ⓑ**

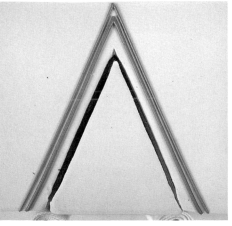

2. Pipe a thinner line beside the piped line. **Ⓐ**

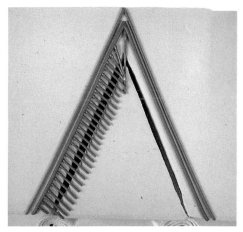

3. Pipe a series of short lines across the wedge-gap shown. **Ⓐ**

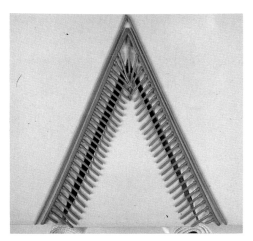

4. Now pipe a series of short lines across the wedge-gap shown. **Ⓐ**

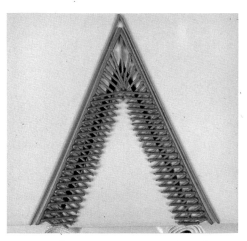

5. Pipe across short lines to form lattice work. **Ⓐ**

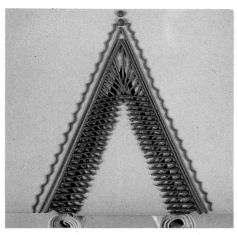

6. Pipe scalloped lines around wedge and then graduated dots at wedge point. **Ⓐ**

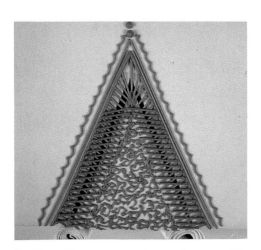

7. Pipe filigree on wedge surface. **Ⓐ**

8. Pipe matching cake-top edge and base pattern on the wedge. Leave to dry for 24 hours. **Ⓚ**

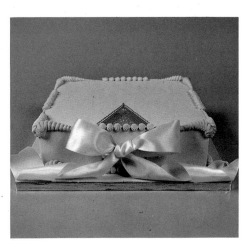

9. Tie wedge ribbon into a bow, then cut and fix bow tails to cake-board.

Before commencing any work on this page, please read the whole sequence of instructions and ensure you have the proper equipment and materials, as well as sufficient time to complete the project. Additional information can be found on pages 6-51 (Index on pages 94-95).

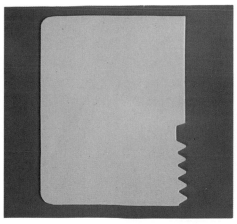

1. Cut (or purchase) a plastic cake scraper to the design shown.

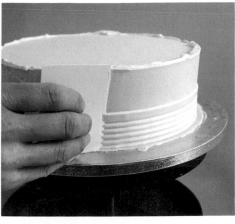

2. Use scraper, as shown, on the final cake-side coating.

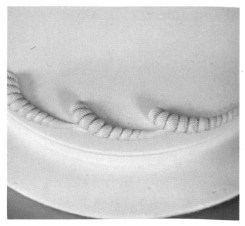

3. Pipe 'C' scrolls around cake-top edge using a star piping tube. **(K)**

4. Pipe shells around cake base. **(K)**

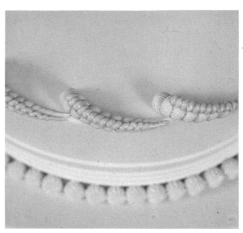

5. Overpipe each 'C' scroll. **(B)**

6. Overpipe shells with a piped line. **(B)**

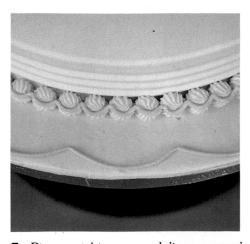

7. Pipe matching curved lines around cake-board. **(B)**

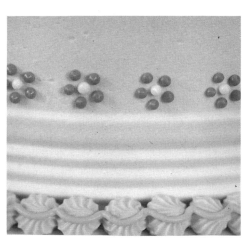

8. Pipe dots around centre of cake-side, as shown. **(B)**

9. Pipe dots around cake-board, as indicated. **(B)**

Note: Royal icing is the medium used on this cake.

Before commencing any work on this page, please read the whole sequence of instructions and ensure you have the proper equipment and materials, as well as sufficient time to complete the project. Additional information can be found on pages 6-51 (Index on pages 94-95).

1. Edible flowers required, such as the japonica illustrated.

2. Thoroughly mix 2 teaspoons of cold water with 1 egg white and then brush mixture on to inside petals of one flower.

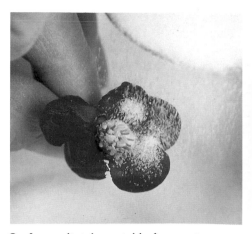

3. Immediately sprinkle fine caster sugar over damp surface. Shake off surplus sugar.

4. Brush mixture on to the back of each petal and immediately sprinkle and remove sugar as before.

5. Repeat this process until sufficient flowers, buds, leaves and twigs have been coated to fully decorate the cake. Leave to dry on greaseproof paper over a wire tray.

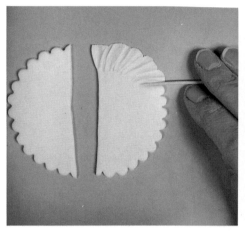

6. Roll out and cut a fluted sugar paste disc, cut in half and then roll each flute with a cocktail stick to form a frill.

7. Place covered cake in position shown on cake-board. Make and fix frills as shown.

8. Pipe graduated bulbs around cake-base along the length of each frill. Ⓑ

9. Arrange and fix (with royal icing) sugar coated flowers, buds and leaves to form a spray.

Before commencing any work on this page, please read the whole sequence of instructions and ensure you have the proper equipment and materials, as well as sufficient time to complete the project. Additional information can be found on pages 6-51 (Index on pages 94-95).

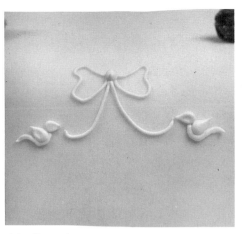

10. Repeat No.9 to form two more sprays on cake-top edge.

11. Pipe the pattern shown on the cake-side between each floral spray. **(A)**

12. Make and fix a sugar paste heart to cake-top centre.

13. Fix sugar-coated japonica twigs and an artificial ring and dove to the heart. Pipe a bow and bulbs around heart. **(A)**

14. Arrange and fix sugar coated japonica sprays to cake-board.

Nature's changing beauty can be captured and preserved, as shown by the sugar coated japonica on this cake. Sugarcraft skills and sugar-coated floral sprays prove to be an admirable combination.

Note: Piped royal icing is used on this sugar-paste coated cake.

Before commencing any work on this page, please read the whole sequence of instructions and ensure you have the proper equipment and materials, as well as sufficient time to complete the project. Additional information can be found on pages 6-51 (Index on pages 94-95).

83

1. Pipe 4 dark coloured heart outlines for each cake tier. **(B)**

2. Flood-in each heart outline with a lighter matching colour. Leave to dry for 24 hours.

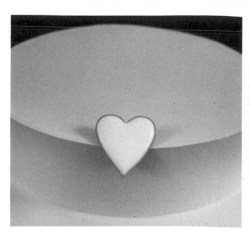

3. Fix a heart (with royal icing) to the cake-top edge at the angle shown.

4. Fix each of the other three hearts at same angle in the positions shown. Leave to dry for 1 hour.

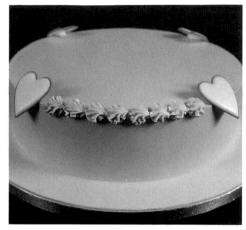

5. Pipe shells along cake-top edge between two hearts. **(F)**

6. Pipe matching number of shells between each pair of hearts. **(F)**

7. Pipe shells around cake-base. **(F)**

8. Fix narrow ribbon around cake-side.

9. Fix artificial decorations of choice around cake and board, as required.

Note: Royal icing is the medium used on this cake

Before commencing any work on this page, please read the whole sequence of instructions and ensure you have the proper equipment and materials, as well as sufficient time to complete the project. Additional information can be found on pages 6-51 (Index on pages 94-95).

1. Outline and flood-in 4 sets of initials of choice for each tier. (A)

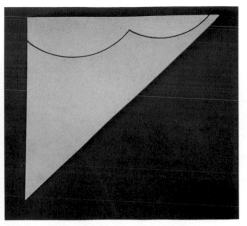

2. Follow instructions on page 45-A and then draw lines, as shown, to form 2 templates, one for the cake top and one for the cake board.

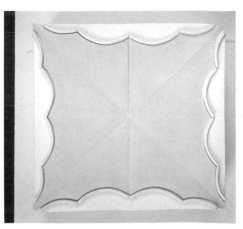

3. Cut along lines, open cake-top template and place in position. Pipe curved lines beside the template, as shown. (C)

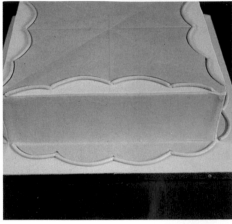

4. Open cake-board templates and place in position shown. Pipe curved lines beside each template, as shown. (C)

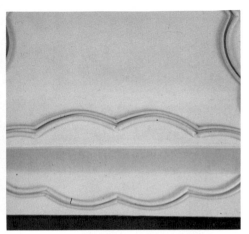

5. Carefully remove templates and pipe a thinner line beside each curved line, as shown. (B)

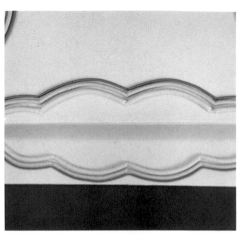

6. Pipe an even thinner line beside each curved line, as shown. (A)

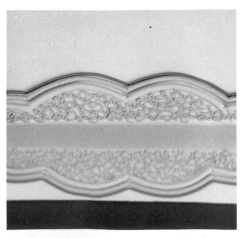

7. Pipe filigree on board and cake-top in the areas indicated. (A)

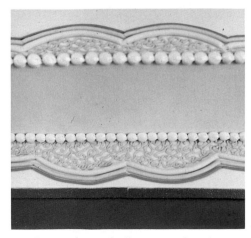

8. Pipe plain shells around cake-top edge and base. (C)

9. Fix initials to cake-sides. Add artificial decorations of choice.

Note: Royal icing is the medium used on this cake

Before commencing any work on this page, please read the whole sequence of instructions and ensure you have the proper equipment and materials, as well as sufficient time to complete the project. Additional information can be found on pages 6-51 (Index on pages 94-95).

Basic Fruit Cake Recipe Table

Note: *This table gives the basic ingredients for a fruit cake in Imperial, Metric and American measures. See key at foot of page.*

AT-A-GLANCE INGREDIENT QUANTITIES CONVERSION

Recipe Multiples	1	× 1½	× 2	× 3	× 4	× 5	× 6	× 7	× 8	
Plain flour	2	3	4	6	8	10	12	14	16	ounces
	57	85	114	170	227	284	340	397	454	grammes
	½	¾	1	1½	2	2½	3	3½	4	cups
Brown sugar	2	3	4	6	8	10	12	14	16	ounces
	57	85	114	170	227	284	340	397	454	grammes
	⅓	½	⅔	1	1⅓	1⅔	2	2⅓	2⅔	cups
Butter	2	3	4	6	8	10	12	14	16	ounces
	57	85	114	170	227	284	340	397	454	grammes
	¼	⅜	½	¾	1	1¼	1½	1¾	2	cups
Currants	2½	3¾	5	7½	10	12½	15	17½	20	ounces
	71	107	142	213	284	355	425	497	568	grammes
	½	¾	1	1½	2	2½	3	3½	4	cups
Sultanas	2½	3¾	5	7½	10	12½	15	17½	20	ounces
	71	107	142	213	284	355	425	497	568	grammes
	½	¾	1	1½	2	2½	3	3½	4	cups
Seedless raisins	1	1½	2	3	4	5	6	7	8	ounces
	28	42	57	85	114	142	170	198	227	grammes
	3	4½	6	9	12	15	18	21	24	tablespoons
Glacé cherries	1	1½	2	3	4	5	6	7	8	ounces
	28	42	57	85	114	142	170	198	227	grammes
	3	4½	6	9	12	15	18	21	24	tablespoons
Mixed peel	1½	2¼	3	4½	6	7½	9	10½	12	ounces
	42	64	85	127	170	213	255	312	340	grammes
	4½	6¾	9	13½	18	22½	27	31½	36	tablespoons
Ground almonds	¾	1⅛	1½	2¼	3	3¾	4½	5¼	6	ounces
	21	32	42	64	85	106	127	149	170	grammes
	2½	3¾	5	7½	10	12½	15	17½	20	tablespoons
Brandy or rum	½	¾	1	1½	2	2½	3	3½	4	fluid ounces
	2	3	4	6	8	10	12	14	16	teaspoons
	2	3	4	6	8	10	12	14	16	teaspoons
Large fresh eggs	1	1½	2	3	4	5	6	7	8	eggs
Nutmeg	1	1½	2	3	4	5	6	7	8	pinches
Mixed spice	1	1½	2	3	4	5	6	7	8	pinches
Salt	1	1½	2	3	4	5	6	7	8	pinches
Lemon zest & juice	¼	⅜	½	¾	1	1¼	1½	1¾	2	lemons
Approx baking time	1½	1¾	2	2½	3	3½	4	4½	5	hours

Baking temperature: 275°F or 135°C or Gas Mark 1

Key: | Imperial | Metric | American | Common Ingredients |

Basic Genoese Recipe Table

Note: *These tables gives the basic ingredients for a Genoese and a sponge cake in Imperial, Metric and American measures. See key at foot of page.*

Tin sizes	8″ round or 7″ square / 20cm round or 18cm square	10″ round or 9″ square / 25cm round or 23cm square	12″ round or 11″ square / 30cm round or 28cm square	inches / centimetres
Butter	1½	3	4½	ounces
	42	85	127	grammes
	3	6	9	tablespoons
Margarine	1½	3	4½	ounces
	42	85	127	grammes
	3	6	9	tablespoons
Caster sugar	3	6	9	ounces
	85	170	255	grammes
	⅜	¾	1⅛	cups
Lightly beaten whole eggs	1½	3	4½	eggs
	1½	3	4½	eggs
	1½	3	4½	eggs
Self raising sieved flour	3	6	9	ounces
	85	170	255	grammes
	¾	1½	2¼	cups
Baking test time	20	22	24	minutes

Baking temperature: 375°F or 190°C or Gas Mark 5

Basic Sponge Recipe Table

Tin sizes (round)	6″ / 15cm	7″ / 18cm	8″ / 20½cm	9″ / 23cm	10″ / 25½cm	inches / centimetres
Eggs	2	2½	3	4	5½	ounces
	57	71	85	113	156	grammes
	½	⅔	¾	1	1⅓	cups
Caster sugar	2	2½	3	4	5½	ounces
	57	71	85	113	156	grammes
	⅓	½	⅔	¾	1	cups
Self raising sieved flour	2	2½	3	4	5½	ounces
	57	71	85	113	156	grammes
	½	⅔	¾	1	1⅓	cups
Hot water	1	1¼	1½	2	2½	teaspoons
	5	6	7½	10	12½	ml
	1	1¼	1½	2	2½	cups
Baking test time	12	13	14	15	16	minutes

Baking temperature: 400°F or 204°C or Gas Mark 6

Key: Imperial   Metric   American

Helpful Hints and Tips

To ensure consistency, always deliberately follow the relevant recipe in this book.

Pre-planning is essential.

Only use the best quality ingredients.

ALMOND PASTE – MAKING

1. Almond paste differs from marzipan in that –
   (a) *Almond Paste* is a mixture of *uncooked* ground almonds, sugar and eggs.
   (b) *Marzipan* is a mixture of *cooked* ground almonds and sugar.
2. In the production of almond paste it is essential that all equipment is thoroughly clean. Personal cleanliness is equally important when handling almond paste.
3. Only use best quality ground almonds.
4. When making almond paste do not overmix, as oil will be squeezed from the almonds and will ruin the almond paste.
5. Under no circumstances should flour come into contact with almond paste.
6. Store almond paste in polythene bags or waxed paper in a cool, dry place.
7. If, after storage, the almond paste is too hard for use, wrap in greaseproof paper and gently warm in oven until pliable.

ALBUMEN SOLUTION – MAKING

1. It is essential that all utensils are completely free from grease and sterilised in boiling water.
2. Albumen solution should only be made from pure dried egg white and water in accordance with the recipe in this book.
3. Pure albumen powder will keep indefinitely, if stored in a cool dry place in a sealed container.
4. Only use cold water when making albumen solution, as warm water will cook the albumen.
5. Made-up albumen solution will keep several days in a sealed container in a refrigerator.

BUTTERCREAM – MAKING

1. To obtain best results, always use best fresh butter.
2. Always sieve icing sugar.
3. Ensure butter is at a temperature of 65-70°F for mixing.
4. If the buttercream is too dense, continue beating until a light fluffy texture is achieved.
5. If buttercream is cold or has been standing for 2/3 days, rewarm to 65-70°F and re-beat before using.
6. To vary the taste and texture of buttercream beat-in any of the following ingredients – whisked egg white, milk, egg, marshmallow, fondant, condensed milk, and edible colours and flavours.
7. The addition of strong artificial food colours tend to give a bitter taste.

BUTTERCREAM – CHOCOLATE FLAVOURED

Add melted chocolate to slightly warmed buttercream and continuously beat the two together. This avoids the chocolate setting and making the buttercream lumpy.

FONDANT – MAKING

1. Perhaps the two most important aspects of making fondant are –
   (a) accurate temperature control; and
   (b) the continual brushing down (with water) of the inside of the saucepan during the whole of the boiling period, to prevent crystal formation.
2. *DO NOT* stir or agitate the fondant in any way whatever once the mixture has reached boiling point.
3. A copper based saucepan is recommended when making fondant.

FONDANT – USING

1. When heating fondant for use, only heat the required amount in a bain-Marie or double saucepan – *NOT* on direct heat.
2. When fondant has reached 95°F/35°C, add stock syrup, if necessary, to attain a coating consistency. (Note: Water can be added instead of stock syrup, but this will affect the final gloss).
3. Continually stir the fondant until it reaches the working temperature of 100°F/38°C, and then *immediately use* after adding any necessary colouring and flavouring.
4. Signs of overheated fondant are –
   (a) too quick setting;
   (b) difficulty in coating the cake;
   (c) loss of gloss; and
   (d) that it sets too hard and becomes brittle.
5. Signs of underheated fondant are –
   (a) it will remain sticky and runny; and
   (b) it will stay soft and not set.
6. If the fondant is seen to reach just over the working temperature, it can be saved by the immediate addition of a little white fat.
7. Surplus fondant can be removed from the bain-Marie or heating pot and stored in a clean container – covering the fondant's surface with cold water (to prevent skin forming). Prior to re-using the fondant remove the water.
8. Constant reheating of fondant will affect the gloss quality.
9. Prior to coating with fondant, ensure that the sponge, genoese or fruit cake (whether or not marzipanned), is completely sealed with boiling apricot purée.
10. Powdered fondant is now available for the person pressed for time.
11. Fondant *is not* water icing. Water icing is a mixture of boiling water and icing sugar.

FRUIT CAKE – BAKING

1. Never bake a cake in a brand new shiny tin. (Bake off the tin's shininess by putting it in a hot oven when empty).
2. A *too hot oven* will produce a cake which has a cracked crusted top and an uncooked centre. It will be very dark in colour and have burnt fruit (which will produce a bitter taste) around its crust.

3. A *too cool oven* will produce a cake which has uncooked fruit, will dry out quickly, have a very thick crust, be pale in colour, will not keep and may go mouldy in storage.

4. If a cake has been baked in the correct temperature but the middle sinks, it could be that there was too much –
   (a) liquid in the batter;
   (b) baking powder;
   (c) sugar; or
   (d) fat.

5. If a baked cake is found to be crumbly, any of the following reasons could be the cause –
   (a) curdled batter;
   (b) overbeating the fat, sugar and eggs;
   (c) undermixing the flour and fruit into the batter;
   (d) insufficient sugar.

FRUIT CAKE – MAKING

1. To avoid a cake misshape or damage, it is important to line the inside of the tin carefully and evenly (see page 11).
2. Do not add egg too quickly to the batter, otherwise it will curdle and result in poor texture, volume, crumb structure and keeping quality.
3. Should the batter start to curdle, a little of the flour or ground almonds can be beaten with the batter to correct it.
4. Ensure flour is stirred thoroughly into the batter before adding the fruit – but do not overmix, as this will toughen the batter. Flour is best mixed-in with a wooden spoon.
5. Overbeaten batter will not support fruit, which will sink during baking.
6. Make sure all cleaned fruit is as dry as possible.
7. When cleaning fruit do not overwash, as this will remove some of the natural sugars.
8. The cake mixture can stand for up to 24 hours in the cake tin before baking, if this is necessary.
9. The cake mixture can be stored in its tin in a refrigerator for short periods exceeding 24 hours PROVIDED no raising agent has been used in the mixture.
10. A cake needs at least three weeks to mature.

GENOESE – BAKING
See instructions for Sponge – Baking.

GENOESE – MAKING

1. Ensure all ingredients, including fats, are 65/70°F immediately prior to mixing.
2. Do not allow mixture to settle on the side or edge of the mixing bowl, otherwise 'streaking' will occur in finished genoese.
3. Fat and sugar must be *well beaten,* otherwise the genoese will have poor texture and volume.
4. *Do not* add egg too quickly to the batter, otherwise it will curdle and result in poor texture, volume, crumb structure and keeping quality.
5. Add any required colours or flavours AFTER the egg has been beaten into the batter.
6. It is important to gently fold-in the flour and not over-mix, as this will make a heavy mixture which will not rise and which will be tough and resulting in poor volume with large holes in the baked genoese.

7. After pouring mixture into the baking tin be sure not to knock or drop the tin, as this will remove essential air from the batter.
8. If a sunflower oil-based margarine is preferred, it can be used straight from the refrigerator.
   The use of unbleached flour may cause the earlier formation of mould in baked products.

GREASEPROOF PAPER PIPING BAGS

1. Only use a strong pure greaseproof paper when making piping bags.
2. Always have spare greaseproof paper piping bags handy *BEFORE* commencing decorative work.
3. The advantages of using greaseproof paper piping bags are –
   (a) that they are cleaner;
   (b) that they are easier to handle;
   (c) the icing flow can be controlled more accurately;
   (d) they can be easily made in large, medium or small sizes to fit the tube being used;
   (e) that several small bags can contain individual made up colours; and
   (f) they are easily disposable without mess.
4. Never overfill a piping bag.

MARZIPANNING A CAKE (with marzipan or almond paste)

1. Properly prepare the cake to receive the marzipan/almond paste by –
   (a) removing the top of a dome shaped cake;
   (b) removing edges of a sunken cake OR bring up to edge level by filling with marzipan;
   (c) removing all burnt fruit from cake-skin;
   (d) ensuring a square cake is properly squared by adding marzipan, if necessary, to each corner;
   (e) filling-in imperfections with marzipan.
2. When rolling marzipan, always use icing sugar or caster sugar for dusting *BUT NEVER USE* flour or cornflour (as this causes fermentation).
3. Always place a cake on the cake-board without fixing it in any way.
4. Ensure the marzipanned cake has a level top and vertical sides.
5. When fixing marzipan to a cake, always use boiling apricot purée (as this should prevent mould or fermentation between the cake and marzipan).
6. Apricot purée is the most suitable fixing agent as it has the least colour and flavour.
7. As marzipan forms a barrier between the cake and the royal icing, it is necessary for it to be of sufficient thickness to prevent discolouration of the royal icing.
8. After marzipanning, it is advisable to leave the cake to stand in a dry room (65°F/18°C) for three to four days.
9. Do not store a marzipanned cake in a sealed plastic container.
10. Natural colour marzipan should be used when the cake is to be coated with sugar paste rather than royal icing.

NATURAL FLOWERS & LEAVES FOR CRYSTALLISING

All natural flowers and leaves may be crystallised in the manner explained on page 82, including apple blossom;

cherry blossom; japonica; pear blossom; pansy; polyanthus; primrose; primula; rose; and violet. These and some others are edible, *HOWEVER, other varieties of flower may not be edible and SHOULD NOT be crystallised and placed on a cake* – SO ALWAYS CHECK FIRST WITH THE APPROPRIATE AUTHORITY.

1. Only pick a good bloom on the day it is to be used.
2. Ensure the flower is dry before commencing crystallisation.
3. Flower petals will not keep unless they are fully and carefully coated in sugar (see page 82).
4. Crystallised flowers should be stored between layers of tissue paper in a cardboard box.
5. With the passage of time, crystallised flowers become brittle and, therefore, should be handled with great care.

ROYAL ICING – COATING

1. Never coat a cake with royal icing unless it has been 'standing' for 24 hours.
2. Always stir the royal icing just before coating a cake.
3. As the cake is difficult to move once icing has commenced, ensure the cake is correctly placed on the cake-board before coating starts.
4. Only use non-ferrous tools when coating and decorating with royal icing.
5. It is preferable for each cake to have at least three thin royal icing coatings. Each coating should be allowed to dry before applying the next.
6. When a coloured coated cake is required, the following sequence is recommended –
   (a) keep the first coat white;
   (b) the second coat should be a pale shade of the colour required; and
   (c) the final coat(s) to be the actual colour required.
7. Coloured royal icing will dry out patchy if each coat hasn't been evenly applied.
8. Before adding a further coat of royal icing, make sure the previous coating has been trimmed smooth.
9. *DO NOT* dip palette knife or straight edge in water when applying royal icing.
10. Stir a drop of cold water into royal icing which is too stiff to easily coat a cake.
11. If brown stains from the cake penetrate the royal icing coatings, remove all royal icing and pour boiling fondant over the marzipan to seal the cake. Re-coat with royal icing in normal way.
12. Each application of royal icing should be done as quickly as possible.
13. Judicious use of a small spirit level will ensure accuracy when coating cakes.
14. If the royal icing on a coated cake cracks when lifted place another cakeboard underneath the existing cakeboard for additional support.
15. High quality coating leads to less decorative needs.

ROYAL ICING – FIGURE PIPING

1. It is recommended that royal icing for figure piping be made with pure albumen powder.
2. Before piping a figure, ensure the royal icing has been made 24 hours previously to the recipe on page 15 and *does not* contain glycerine.

3. Before figure piping, ensure the royal icing is soft but firm enough to hold its shape.
4. Plan ahead each stage of the figure to be piped and pipe accordingly. (For example, pipe a shirt before a tie, or, the head before the hair).
5. Each stage of icing must be joined to another stage – with no gaps – to form a complete figure (otherwise parts of the figure will become detached when removing it from the waxed paper).
6. Only use small piping bags for figure piping.
7. To avoid producing a flat figure, it is necessary to increase pressure on the piping bag to build up face features (e.g. nose, cheeks and chin – as illustrated on page 48) and other contours.
8. When completed, put the figure in a warm (65°F/18°C), dry place, for quick drying. (CAUTION: In periods of high humidity, longer drying times may be necessary).
9. If preferred, a figure can be piped in white icing, left to dry and then painted with edible food colouring.

ROYAL ICING (GLACÉ ICING) MAKING

1. Strict compliance in following the recipe in this book will ensure the production of perfect royal icing, which can, in the hands of a craftsman, prove to be the premier medium in cake icing artistry.
2. Only make royal icing with fresh egg-white or albumen solution, as this gives the best result. (Substitute albumen does not give such good results).
3. Royal icing is a form of meringue and, therefore, must be well beaten. Failure to do so can result in heavy and difficult-to-handle icing which may set very hard.
4. Over-beaten royal icing – usually by high speed machine – injects too much air into the mixture and causes it to become very fluffy.
5. Whiter than white royal icing can be obtained by adding a small amount of edible blue food colouring in the final mixing stage.
6. It is essential that all utensils are completely free from grease and be sterilised in boiling water.
7. When separating egg-white from yolk, it is very important to ensure that *NO YOLK* enters the royal icing mixture. (Yolk entering the mixture will prevent aeration).
8. Do not add lemon juice to the royal icing mixture, as this will have a discolouring effect.
9. Poorly aerated royal icing can be improved during mixing by adding a small drop of acetic acid. However, *DO NOT* add acetic acid if colouring is to be used.
10. To make 'easy-to-cut' royal icing, add glycerine in accordance with the 'Glycerine – Table for use' instructions on page 15.
11. Always keep royal icing protected by storing it in an air-tight plastic container or covering it with a damp cloth. This will prevent the crusting of the royal icing.
12. Properly stored, royal icing will remain in good condition for two to three weeks. If, when needed, it is found to be too soft, beat in additional icing sugar.
13. Longer periods of storage can be attained by placing the icing in an air-tight plastic container and placing it in a refrigerator. *NOTE:* When removed from the refrigerator for use, it is necessary to allow the royal icing to reach room temperature (65°F/18°C).
14. After making royal icing, always identify whether or not it

contains glycerine (by sticking a label on the plastic container) and also add the date it is made.

ROYAL ICING – PIPING

1. If the royal icing is too stiff to pipe easily and makes the piping-hand ache, remove from bag and beat-in a drop of cold water to obtain a light and stable consistency.
2. If the royal icing is too soft (where the definition of the piped design is lost or doesn't adhere to the cake-edge), remove from bag and beat-in sufficient icing sugar to obtain a light and stable consistency.
3. Always pipe on to a dry coated cake as any error can then easily be scraped off.
4. It is advisable to use two hands when piping. One hand exerts bag pressure whilst the other hand guides the tube.
5. When in doubt, practice the piping before applying the design to the cake.
6. When over-piping (piping royal icing on top of piped royal icing), make sure the previous piped work is dry enough to support the additional icing.
7. To ensure accuracy of colour(s), always make up sufficient royal icing to complete any one cake.
8. When not in use, keep filled icing bag tube tips moist, by covering them with a damp cloth or sponge.
9. *DO NOT* use a pin or needle to clear a blocked piping tube. The tube should be removed and washed in warm water.
10. Leave used tubes overnight in cold water to allow adhered sugar to dissolve.

ROYAL ICING – RUNOUTS

1. It is recommended that royal icing for runouts be made with pure albumen powder.
2. Before making a runout, ensure the royal icing has been made 24 hours previously to the recipe on page 15 and *does not* contain glycerine.
3. To convert royal icing for runout filling work, fold in sufficient cold water to achieve a dropping consistency (as illustrated on page 46). Remember, too much additional water will prevent the runout from setting.
4. Only use good quality waxed paper, which should be smooth, thin and as transparent as possible. If only waxed on one side, ensure the runout is on the waxed side.
5. A runout working surface should be hard and smooth, such as a glazed tile or a small sheet of glass.
6. Before filling a piping bag with runout royal icing, tap the container on the table to bring air bubbles to the surface.
7. A piped runout outline must be complete (to avoid the filling from seeping through).
8. When filled, put the runout in a warm (65°F/18°C), dry place, for quick drying. (CAUTION: In periods of high humidity, longer drying times may be necessary).
9. Although runouts can be made well ahead of need, they must be stored in a cardboard box in a dry and warm atmosphere.

SPONGE – BAKING

1. Care should be taken in preparing the sponge tin – see page 6.
2. A *too hot oven* will produce a sponge which is of poor volume (too thin), flavour and shape and is highly

coloured and crusted. This often produces a cake with an uncooked centre bearing numerous holes.
3. A *too cool oven* will produce a sponge which is pale, coarse and has a thick outer crust and which will go stale very quickly.

SPONGE – MAKING

1. All equipment must be grease-free, as grease will attack the batter and result in a no-volume heavy sponge.
2. Do not over-whisk egg and sugar, as this will cause the batter to collapse.
3. It is important to gently fold-in the flour and not over-mix, as this will make a heavy mixture which will not rise and which will be tough.
4. Do not allow mixture to settle on the side or edge of the mixing bowl, otherwise 'streaking' will occur in finished sponge.
5. After pouring mixture into the baking tin be sure not to knock or drop the tin, as this will remove essential air from the batter.
6. After pouring batter into the tin, *do not* spread with any implement. If necessary, tilt tin to spread the batter evenly over the base of the whole tin.
7. Bake immediately batter is poured into the tin.

SUGAR PASTE – MAKING

1. There are a great variety of sugar paste recipes and so the one on page 16 is for general use.
2. In the production of sugar paste it is essential that all equipment be thoroughly clean. Personal cleanliness is equally important when handling sugar paste.
3. Sugar paste should be made 24 hours before use.
4. Accuracy in the use of glucose is a vital aspect in making sugar paste.
5. If the sugar paste is found to be too dry by – not rolling out easily; cracking; and/or will not shape or mould – add a little white fat or egg-white to the mixture.
6. If the sugar paste is too sticky, a little cornflour or icing sugar can be added to the mixture.
7. Sugar paste should be stored in air-tight plastic container in a cool dry place, but *not* in a refrigerator.
8. If the sugar paste has formed a crust, *REMOVE* the crust before use.

Index/Glossary

101 Cake Designs

ISBN: 0 946429 00 6   320 pages
The original Mary Ford definitive cake artistry text book. A classic in its field, over 250,000 copies sold.

The Beginners Guide To Cake Decorating

ISBN: 0 946429 38 3   256 pages
This book assumes no previous experience and covers the basic techniques and recipes before progressing to over 150 cake designs for different occasions.

Chocolate Cookbook

ISBN: 0 946429 18 9   96 pages
A complete introduction to cooking with chocolate featuring sweets, luscious gateaux, rich desserts and Easter Eggs.

Jams, Chutneys and Pickles

ISBN: 0 946429 33 2   96 pages
Over 70 of Mary Ford's favourite recipes for delicious jams, jellies, pickles and chutneys with hints and tips for perfect results.

Sugarpaste Cake Decorating

ISBN: 0 946429 10 3   96 pages
27 innovative Mary Ford cake designs illustrating royal icing decoration on sugarpaste covered cakes.

Children's Cakes

ISBN: 0 946429 35 9   96 pages
33 exciting new Mary Ford designs and templates for children's cakes in a wide range of mediums.

Party Cakes

ISBN: 0 946429 09 X   120 pages
36 superb party time sponge cake designs and templates for tots to teenagers. An invaluable prop for the party cake decorator.

Sugar Flowers Cake Decorating

ISBN: 0 946429 12 X   96 pages
Practical, easy-to-follow pictorial instructions for making and using superb, natural looking sugar flowers for cakes.

Decorative Sugar Flowers for Cakes

ISBN: 0 946429 28 6   120 pages
33 of the highest quality handcrafted sugar flowers with cutter shapes, background information and appropriate uses.

Sugarcraft Cake Decorating

ISBN: 0 946429 30 8   96 pages
A definitive sugarcraft book featuring an extensive selection of exquisite sugarcraft items designed and made by Pat Ashby.

Making Glove Puppets

ISBN: 0 946429 26 X   96 pages
14 specially designed fun glove puppets with full size templates and step-by-step instructions for each stage.

Home Baking with Chocolate

ISBN: 0 946429 37 5   96 pages
Over 60 tried and tested recipes for cakes, gateaux, biscuits, confectionary and desserts. The ideal book for busy mothers.

Desserts

ISBN: 0 946429 40 5   96 pages
Hot and cold desserts suitable for every occasion using fresh, natural ingredients. An invaluable reference book for the home cook, student or chef.

The Complete Book of Cake Decorating

ISBN: 0 946429 36 7   256 pages
An indispensable reference book for cake decorators, containing totally new material covering every aspect of cake design and artistry.